The Crozier and the Dáil

Church and State in Ireland 1922-1986

by John Cooney

THE MERCIER PRESS LTD

The Mercier Press Limited
4 Bridge Street, Cork.
24 Lower Abbey Street, Dublin 1.

First edition 1986
Cover design by Eddie McManus
Typeset by Alphaset, Limerick
Printed by Litho Press, Midleton

ISBN 0 85342 782 8

Contents

Note: The *Dáil* is the Irish parliament which meets at Leinster House, Dublin.
The *Oireachtas* is the legislative process comprising Dáil, Senate and the President.

PROLOGUE: GARRET'S CRUSADE

27th September, 1981

Dr Garret FitzGerald meant it to be described as a constitutional initiative to persuade the public of the need to remove laws and institutions which had made the Irish Republic "a sectarian State." But during a radio interview with Mr Gerry Barry the Taoiseach said he wanted to lead "a republican crusade." The word "crusade" had been used earlier by Mr Brian Lenihan of Fianna Fáil to describe Dr FitzGerald's approach: for better or worse, the term "Garret's Crusade" stuck.

"I believe passionately in a united Ireland and I believe in the principles enunciated by Tone and Davis. I came into politics for two reasons in 1965. I had seen in previous decades this State develop along lines which Tone and Davis would have abhorred, a State that was not the non-sectarian State that they had sought to establish.

"It had become a State imbued by the majority of people who lived in that part of Ireland. I saw this country become partitioned by constitutions and laws which were alien to the people of Ireland as a whole.

"I became increasingly concerned to get into politics about that. I entered politics for that purpose and to try to achieve social reforms and to eliminate poverty from this country.

"I believe that this part of the country has slipped into a partitionist attitude with institutions which are acceptable to people living down here but could never be the basis to enter discussions with unionists in Northern Ireland.

"I can't accept this. I'm from the North. My mother came from a northern Presbyterian family and from her and my father, a southern Catholic, I have inherited this belief in the republic of Tone and Davis.

"We have created here something which the northern Protestants find unacceptable. I believe it is my job to try and lead our people to understand how it is that we have divided this island.

7

"It is the changes we have made in our laws that have differentiated us and made our State unacceptable to a part of the Irish people who could be reconciled. And I know they could.

"What I want to do is to lead a crusade — a republican crusade, — to make this a genuine Republic on the principles of Tone and Davis, and, if I can, bring the people of this country on that path and get them to agree down here to the type of state that Tone and Davis looked for.

"I believe we could have the basis then on which many Protestants in Northern Ireland would be willing to consider a relationship with us, who at present have no reason to do so".

"If I was a northern Protestant today, I can't see how I could aspire to getting involved in a State which is itself sectarian in the acutely sectarian way Northern Ireland was in which Catholics were repressed.

"Our laws, constitutions and our practices are not acceptable to the Protestants of Northern Ireland.

"My job is to persuade the Irish people to adopt the principles of Tone and Davis.

"I know that Fianna Fáil don't believe in them. I know that Mr. de Valera in 1931 opposed the appointment of a librarian in Co. Mayo on the grounds that she was a Protestant.

"I know that in 1979 the present leader of the opposition introduced a Bill on contraception in the Dáil which used theological language of one Church in a sectarian way on the contraception issue — so little does he understand or care for the sensibilities of the people of Northern Ireland".

On the question of a referendum on a new constitution and its timing, Dr. FitzGerald said: "I'm not going to rush into a referendum before people have time to think about the realities I'm putting to them".

"My job is to lead people to a point where they see the need to make the changes, to have a new constitution which would be the kind of constitution which Tone and Davis wanted in this country. If I can bring the people of this State to such a position of commitment to a united Ireland, I will certainly bring the matter to the people. I hope I can win this crusade".

The Taoiseach said he would move on a referendum on a new constitution once he felt there was sufficient support for the initiative, and he would do so with or without the support of Fianna Fáil.

"If the people of this country decide they prefer a 26 county State based on the majority ethos, and they are not prepared to work with the people of Northern Ireland towards unity on a basis that would be common to both, I would accept defeat and leave politics at that stage if necessary.

"But I am certainly going to use what political life I have ahead of me to try and achieve this because that's what I came into politics to do.

"I hope I can do so. I hope I can bring public opinion with me on this. I hope to recreate the genuine and true republicanism in Ireland that we have inherited from the past and that we have rejected in this State over the past 60 years right up to that Bill in 1979.

"I will try and bring the people along this road and if I can get them to do so then certainly a new constitution will be put before the people.

"If it is evident that the people are not prepared to follow and that they have been brainwashed for so long by Fianna Fáil into this partitionist State based on the ethos of the majority and that I can't change that and that a new referendum was likely to fail, then it would convince people in Northern Ireland that there's simply no point in pursuing the question of a new relationship with us.

"I'm afraid that one of the problems in this is the other political party, Fianna Fáil. So few of them have been willing to go north and talk to people. Look at the number of visits made by Fianna Fáil ministers. They know nothing of Northern Ireland. They haven't been there. They haven't met any of the people.

"I've spent my life meeting Protestant and Catholic. I know many are desperately anxious for a solution. How many, if we could create a State down here which we would accept and in which they could find the civil and religious liberties they believe in, would be willing to think again about this?.

Chapter 1

THE CATHOLIC STATE

To accuse Fianna Fáil of betraying Wolfe Tone, as Garret FitzGerald did in his radio interview in September 1981, was bound to enrage its leader, Charles Haughey. Wolfe Tone (1763-1798), was a founder member of the Society of United Irishmen which aimed "to break the connection with England" and to unite "Protestant, Catholic and Dissenter in the common name of Irishmen". Charles Haughey was the politican who less than a year before, as Taoiseach, had opened up "the totality of relationships" between Britain and Ireland for discussion at a Dublin Castle Summit with Prime Minister, Margaret Thatcher. Haughey was — and still is — convinced that Northern Ireland is a "failed entity" and that the way forward is for the British and Irish Governments to convene a constitutional conference involving all the democratic political parties north and south to work out a new constitution for a 32 county Ireland.

On many occasions Mr. Haughey has assured unionists that Fianna Fáil would be generous in its acceptance of a constitution that would embrace all types of belief and identity, but he has been equally insistent that any diminution of the Republic's aspirations for a united Ireland in advance of negotiations at an all-round constitutional conference would weaken its bargaining position. Thus Mr. Haughey accused Dr. FitzGerald of sabotaging the policy of national unity and of giving unionists propaganda with which to gloat at the southern State. In particular Mr. Haughey made it clear that he would oppose any attempt by Dr. FitzGerald to remove articles two and three from the Republic's constitution, relating to the territorial claims on Northern Ireland as part of the whole of Ireland.

What added insult to injury was the coincidence that Dr. FitzGerald broadcast his constitutional crusade on a Sunday on which Fianna Fáil, in veneration as the inheritors of Tone's Republican ideals, was visiting his grave in the churchyard at Bodenstown, Co Kildare. The coincidence was not missed by the leader writer in *The Irish Times* who commented "on the day that Fianna Fáil chose to visit Bodenstown, he more than they, will have caused the bones of Wolfe Tone to rock with joy and anticipation. Now the Fine Gael leader has openly run up the Bodenstown colours and has stolen from Fianna Fáil something which the older generation of men in that party cherished".

The furore which Dr. FitzGerald's passionate plea provoked was proof that he was touching live nerves in the society of the 26 counties. Had he been denouncing the sectarian moulds of Irish society over the past 60 years from the vantage point of an academic, Dr. FitzGerald's comments would have been regarded by many as a statement of historical orthodoxy. But he was speaking as Taoiseach; he was implicitly criticising his predecessors in that lofty office - and above all, he was promising to do something to reverse this trend or quit politics. Nor was he underestimating the strength of the forces which had shaped the outlook of the south over six decades.

Under the influence of British liberal thought, the 1922 constitution of the newly created Free State was a secular one. The Catholic Church was not even mentioned, let alone its status defined. There was no official alliance between the State and the Church: bishops and priests were not invited to participate in either government or parliament. No politician proclaimed his new State to be Catholic. Officially, Home Rule was neither Rome Rule nor clerical rule.

But as Dr. Conor Cruise O'Brien, in his *States of Ireland,* has noted, "the affairs of the new State were not long administered in a purely secular spirit". The predominant values were imbued in the people by Mother Church, whose bishops had supported the pro-Treaty side during the Civil War and who now formed part of the new establishment. There was therefore a clear incentive, if not temptation, for the Cumann na nGaedheal government of W.T. Cosgrave to woo bishops and priests, especially if in doing so they tarred the bona fides of de Valera and the anti-Treaty Republicans who had been excommunicated during the Civil War by the Catholic Church authorities. By the same token, there was the drive in de Valera, encouraged by influential churchmen such as Monsignor John Hagan of the Irish College in Rome and Archbishop Daniel Mannix, to become respectable in the eyes of the Catholic bishops. In his pioneering study, *The Vatican, the bishops and Irish politics, 1919-39,* Dr. Dermot Keogh has revealed how Monsignor Hagan convinced de Valera of the need for a new departure in politics which would make Fianna Fáil "a constitutional alternative to Cumann na nGaedheal, even if some of the Fianna Fáil backbenchers were inclined to a 'slightly constitutional' position, as they maintained a rather ambivalent attitude towards the IRA and the use of violence in relation to Northern Ireland".

According to Dr. Keogh, Fianna Fáil may officially have been launched as a political party in the La Scala Theatre in Dublin in April 1926, but "it can be argued that the decision to found Fianna Fáil was probably taken in the Irish College in Rome". Mr. de Valera would seek to outflank Cosgrave in the bid for clerical support and favour.

Nor was the Catholic Church diffident about gaining and exercising influence on society. Years later in his colourful memoirs the late Tod Andrews wrote "of the lengths to which the Church would go to maintain its dominance of a peasant population steeped in superstition and an urban proletariat soused in Saint Joseph's medals, Saint Blaise's flannel and a dozen different varieties of scapulars".

In understanding the hierarchy's partitionist mentality, however, it should be recalled that in the mid-nineteenth century the Irish Catholic Church had become Romanised during the long pontificate of Pope Pius IX which culminated in Vatican Council One's declaration in 1870 of papal infallibility. The main agent for exposing the Irish Church to these ultramontane, or Romanising trends was Archbishop Paul Cullen of Dublin. Lost sight of was Daniel O'Connell's concept of a free church in a free state, so admired by French liberal Catholics such as Lamennais, Lacordaire and Montalembert. Increasingly the barque of St. Patrick was tied to the barque of Peter which claimed the exclusive right to issue administrative orders to the crew.

Partition virtually coincided with the election in February 1922 of Achille Ratti as Pope Pius XI, a man born to command (nato per il comando) who ruled over the Catholic Church until 1939 in an authoritarian, even autocratic manner which was made more efficient by the developments in communications. This style of monarchical government was effortlessly continued by his successor, the austere Eugenio Pacelli, who reigned as Pope Pius XII until 1958. Consequently, the fledgling Irish State began to formulate its policies and develop its institutions in a period which saw the papacy scale new heights of centralised certitude.

An important instance of the mood in Rome was the response of Pius XI to the pioneering and exciting talks on church unity which took place in Malines, Belgium, from 1921 onwards, between Archbishop Désiré Joseph Mercier and the Church of England group led by Lord Halifax. Such talks were defined by Pius as a complete failure and he described ecumenism as being valid only in the context of "separated brethren" returning to the true faith in the Roman Catholic Church. Preaching that there was no eternal salvation for those outside the Catholic Church, Irish bishops and priests taught a docile laity to obey the commandments of the Church as well as the ten commandments. The Church made it clear to the politicians that it was their duty to ensure that legislation should direct men and women to live a moral life and that Catholic values should permeate society. Catholic doctrine was impressed deeply in the consciousness of Irish politicians in regard to matters of public and private morality. The years 1922 onwards imprinted that ethical code into the official actions of the new State.

Dr. Keogh's research has convinced him that consultation was an integral part of the relationship between Catholic churchmen and politicians since the foundation of the State, though such discussions were very often informal and unstructured, reflecting a "closed government" approach which produced a system of politics of informal consensus. But such consensus increasingly rested not on Wolfe Tone's common name of Irishmen but on the sociological fact that partition put three-quarters of all Protestants in the jurisdiction of the Northern Ireland State. In other words, only about one in ten citizens of the Free State was not a Catholic. Of a total population of 2,971,992 in the 1926 census, 2,751,269 were Catholics. From eight per cent of the Free State's population in 1926 the Protestant population was to shrink to below three per cent in the 1970s largely as the result of migration from a State whose ethos was deemed to be too Catholic, from a lower birth rate among Protestants compared with Catholics and, most controversially from the adverse effect of the Catholic *Ne Temere* decree on mixed marriages, which was in force until 1970 when it was modified by Pope Paul VI.

Although the island had been divided into Orange and Green States, the territorial jurisdiction of the Catholic Church — as indeed of the main Protestant Churches — remained on an all-Ireland basis. But as historian, Michael Laffan, points out, "the Catholic nature of independent Ireland was never sought by nationalists but once it had been imposed and had become a fact of life many people were attracted by the opportunity of building a more thoroughly Catholic State than a united Ireland could ever have become".

From the start politicians in the 26 counties exercised State power to promote and defend Catholic moral values. In the State Paper Office in Dublin Castle there is a letter dated February 24th, 1921, containing a proposal from Mr. W.T. Cosgrave to Mr. de Valera. An accompanying note explained that the suggestion was "that there should be a sort of Upper House to the Dáil consisting of a theological board which would decide whether any enactments of the Dáil were contrary to faith and morals or not. There is also a suggestion that a guarantee be given to the Holy Father that the Dáil will not make laws contrary to the teaching of the Church, in return for which the Holy Father will be asked to recognise the Dáil as a body entitled to legislate for Ireland".

But a civil servant commented wisely: "I am afraid that in practice the theological board would not work and might lead to very grave trouble. Besides, for the Dáil to admit that there existed a necessity for such a check on their legislation would, I think, be a fatal error". Nothing came of this proposal. Nor was action taken on a Free State Government plan to endow the Archdiocese of Dublin with the site of the General Post

Office in O'Connell Street, where the 1916 Rising had taken place, for the building of a cathedral.

If such pious schemes failed to materialise, the new State had little hesitation in accepting and enforcing Catholic teaching on matters such as divorce and contraception and used censorship to cultivate a closed society, reinforced by strong Church control of the education system, a system which satisfied the minority Protestant community because it had its own separate schools which were endowed financially by the State. For decades "a clerical garb, in a clerical school" was deemed to be sufficient qualifications for a teacher.

In an address to the Patrick MacGill Summer School, in August 1985, Dr. Noel Browne referred to Peadar O'Donnell's famous remark that "we are not a cleric ridden country, it is a yahoo ridden church". If by that O'Donnell meant that clerics were harrassed by a yahoo laity, Dr. Browne asked, "how can those who educate that laity,that is Rome, to behave as yahoos, escape the blame for their subsequent behaviour?"

Divorce

The divorce issue provides a classic case study in "the politics of informal consensus". Although divorce had been permitted under the Brehon laws, there were no divorce courts in Ireland during the union with Britain. Wealthy couples however could petition the Westminster Parliament for the initiation and enactment of private members' bills to obtain dissolution of marriages with the right to remarry. The maintenance of "this little luxury" for the minority Protestant community in the Free State was privately mooted in 1923 by the Attorney General, Hugh Kennedy. This received a frosty response from W.T. Cosgrave. A minister, Edmund Duggan, was authorised to sound out the view of the Archbishop of Dublin, Dr. Edward Byrne who indicted that the hierarchy would oppose any move to allow the Oireachtas to handle such private members' bills.

When it was pointed out to Dr. Byrne that removal of this divorce facility would persuade more Protestants to leave the Free State, he retorted that its maintenance would be construed as acceptance in principle of divorce by the bishops. "Ireland would not lose anything" by their departure.

15

Despite these indications from the episcopal palace in Drumcondra, Mr. Kennedy stuck to his opinion that the withdrawal of the divorce facility from the Oireachtas' standing orders would be seen by Protestants as an invasion of their rights which the Catholic majority had pledged to defend. He therefore proposed that the private members' bill procedure could be retained without specific Oireachtas reference to divorce. Even this compromise foundered when Mr. Cosgrave sent the suggestion to Dr. Byrne, who in turn raised the matter at a meeting of the hierarchy in Maynooth.

A curt reply, signed by Cardinal Logue of Armagh, read: "Hitherto, in obedience to the divine law, no divorce with right to remarry has ever been granted in this country. The bishops of Ireland have to say that it would be altogether unworthy of an Irish legislative body to sanction concessions of such divorce, no matter who the petitioners may be".

The consultations between Mr. Cosgrave and the bishops had taken place in private - but are recorded in Dr. Ronan Fanning's masterly study of *Independent Ireland* - before any petitioner had attempted to initiate the procedure. The test came in 1925 when three private members' bills were tabled before the Oireachtas. In an angry reaction to these requests, Cosgrave pushed through the Dáil a motion preventing the introduction in future of such bills. "The majority of the people of this country regard the bond of marriage as a sacramental bond which is incapable of being dissolved", he told the Dáil. "I personally hold this view. I consider that the whole fabric of our social organisation is based upon the sanctity of the marriage bond and that anything that tends to weaken the binding efficacy of that bond to that extent strikes at the root of our social life".

The outstanding opponent of the Dáil motion was Professor W.E. Thrift, a Protestant who was an independent deputy representing Trinity College, Dublin. "I regard this motion as one which will have the effect of imposing on the whole population the religious views, in respect of divorce, of the majority of the population", he said, going on to recall the promises made to Protestants by Arthur Griffith during the Treaty debates in 1922. "I cannot but feel that in this motion I see the first sign - I will not say it is the prelude to others - of what is

16

not fair play to all sections of the community ... I wish to lay my principal stress on liberty of thought and independence of conscience".

Professor Thrift stressed the class discrimination contained in Cosgrave's motion because the wealthy could live outside the State for a period and obtain a divorce in Britain or elsewhere but poorer people could not afford that mobility. "The passing of this motion will raise up one more barrier against a possible union between the north of Ireland and the south of Ireland", he warned.

Although another of Trinity's three deputies, Henry Alton, agreed that the motion would preclude "ourselves from giving the minority the opportunity of redress they at present possess", the mood of the Dáil was distinctly anti-divorce. Professor John Marcus O'Sullivan denied that the issue involved individual liberty. "I do not believe it is any more within the competence of the Dáil or any government or legislature to pass legislation for the dissolution of the marriage tie than it is to pass legislation for the beheading of red-haired men", he said. Vice-President Kevin O'Higgins, who was to be assassinated two years later, said that the Dáil was not competent to discuss divorce and that it had better rid itself of its rights. A Labour deputy, Bill Davin, described those who sought a divorce as being people without consciences. The Minister for Finance, Ernest Blythe, a northern Protestant, argued that the motion would not make partition permanent. "That is trying to lift the matter into a question of high politics - trying to make it a big political question as distinct from a social or religious question", he said, arguing that there was no constitutional right to divorce.

The motion was carried in the Dáil and came before the upper house, the Senate, on June 11th, 1925, when the poet W.B. Yeats delivered a brilliant speech which was regarded as highly offensive by his Catholic colleagues: "It is perhaps the deepest political passion with this nation that north and south be united into one nation. If it ever comes that north and south unite, the north will not give up any liberty which she already possesses under her constitution. You will then have to grant to another people what you refuse to grant those within your borders. If you show that this country, southern

Ireland, is going to be governed by Catholic ideas and by Catholic ideas alone, you will never get the north. You will create an impassable barrier between south and north, and you will pass more and more Catholic laws, while the north will, gradually, assimilate its divorce and other laws to those of England. You will put a wedge into the midst of this nation".

Yeats, taunted with the fact that the Church of Ireland Bishop of Meath had spoken in favour of the abolition of divorce, went on: "...If the entire Protestant episcopacy of Ireland came out with a declaration on this subject, it would not influence a vote in this House. It is one of the glories of the Church in which I was born that we have put our bishops in their places in discussions requiring legislation".

"Even in those discussions involving legislation of matters of religion they count only according to their individual intelligence and knowledge. The rights of divorce and many other rights were won by the Protestant communities in the teeth of the most bitter opposition from the clergy. The living, changing, advancing human mind sooner or later refuses to accept this legislation from men who base their ideas on the interpretation of doubtful texts in the Gospels..."

"I think it is tragic that within three years of this country gaining its independence we should be discussing a measure which a minority of this nation considers to be grossly oppressive. I am proud to consider myself a typical man of that minority. We against whom you have done this thing are no petty people. We are one of the great stocks of Europe. We are the people of Burke; we are the people of Grattan; we are the people of Swift, the people of Emmet, the people of Parnell. We have created the most of the modern literature of this country. We have created the best of its political intelligence. Yet I do not altogether regret what has happened. I shall be able to find out, if not I, my children will be able to find out whether we have lost our stamina or not. You have defined our position and given us a popular following. If we have not lost our stamina then your victory will be brief, and your defeat final, and when it comes this nation may be transformed."

Next day, *The Irish Times,* then the Protestant newspaper,

18

commented: "The problems of reconciling the minority's constitutional freedom with the dictates of the majority's conscience is by far the most delicate problem with which this State has been, is, or ever is likely to be, confronted. Yet it must be solved if the Free State's very name is not to be a lie, if a rankling sense of injustice is not to be a canker at the very root of progress, and if the nation's hopes for a United Ireland ever are to be fulfilled. For the solution of this problem, the country's and the legislature's highest gifts of heart and brain will be required — statesmanship, patience, ingenuity and above all, understanding and tolerance".

The Catholicisation of the Free State proceeded at a steady pace: in 1923 a law was approved on film censorship; in 1924 and 1927 laws curtailing the consumption of strong alcoholic drink were introduced, at the prompting of the bishops, despite the obvious national fondness for drink; the 1929 Censorship of Publications Act set up a vigilante committee of five censors, one a priest, three Catholic lay persons and a Protestant. The process described by Dr. John Whyte, author of *Church and State in Modern Ireland, 1923-79,* of enshrining the Catholic moral code in the law of the State continued at the same vigorous pace under Fianna Fáil governments headed by Mr. de Valera from 1932 onwards, culminating in the passage of the 1937 Constitution.

"Mr. Cosgrave," Dr. Whyte writes, "refused to legalise divorce; Mr. de Valera made it unconstitutional. Mr. Cosgrave's government regulated films and books; Mr. de Valera's regulated dance halls. Mr. Cosgrave's government forbade propaganda for the use of contraceptives; Mr. de Valera's banned their sale or import. In all this they had the support of the third party in Irish politics, the Labour party. The Catholic populace gave no hint of protest. The Protestant minority acquiesced. The only real opposition came from a coterie of literary men whose impact on public opinion was slight".

1937 Constitution

In 1925 de Valera said, "Ireland remains a Catholic nation, and as such, sets the eternal destiny of man above the issues and idols of the day". De Valera confirmed his own stature as a Catholic statesman with his replacement of the liberal 1922 constitution with the more Catholic-inspired constitution of 1937. On his initiative, and after consultations with both Catholic and Protestant churchmen, de Valera inserted a clause recognising "the special position" of the Holy, Catholic, Apostolic and Roman Church, while also recognising the existence in the State of the Protestant and Jewish communities. In a conversation with the Church of Ireland Archbishop of Dublin, Dr. George Allen Gregg, Mr. de Valera assured him that the term "special position" was merely descriptive and did not confer legal rights. Incidentally, it was Dr. Gregg who had brought to Mr. de Valera's attention the fact that the decrees of the Council of Trent described the Roman Catholic Church as "the Holy, Catholic, Apostolic and Roman Church". Despite representations from Cardinal MacRory of Armagh, de Valera used the phrase Church of Ireland to describe Anglicanism.

The constitution, which states that all authority is from the Most Holy Trinity, reflected Catholic teaching on the family, marriage and education as well as on social matters such as the rights of private property. But the 1922 provisions on religious liberty and non-endowment of religion remained in the 1937 constitution, much to the chagrin of ultra-conservative politicians and groups who would have liked, as especially did Dr. MacRory, to see reference to the Catholic religion as "established by our Divine Lord Jesus Christ".

As befitted a Catholic statesman, de Valera sought papal approval in competition to Cardinal MacRory who was urging Pope Pius XI that it was not Catholic enough. Pius XI neither condemned nor confirmed it, but a political victory "was won by de Valera when *L'Osservatore Romano* published a favourable comment on the constitution which, not surprisingly, appeared in *The Irish Press:* "It differs from other constitutions, because it is inspired by respect for the faith of the people, the dignity of the person, the sanctity of the family, of private property, and of social democracy. These principles are applied in a unique religious spirit, which animates the whole constitution". Even greater approbation of the constitution was forthcoming from the Secretary of State, Cardinal Pacelli, soon to be Pope Pius XII, who viewed it as a model Constitution. It is a mixture of Thomist and Scholastic philosophy, with a large measure of social policy derived from papal encyclicals.

The Mother and Child Scheme

The relationship between the Irish State and the hierarchy also had its moments of disagreement. A potential crisis loomed for Fianna Fáil in 1947 as a result of a Health Act which it had introduced enabling the State to provide for the health of all children, to prepare women for motherhood and to provide all women with gynaecological care. The coming to power in 1948 of an inter-party government averted a conflict between the hierarchy and Mr. de Valera. The inheritor of the brewing problem was Dr. Noel Browne, the young and enterprising Minister for Health who was appointed to this office by the leader of the radical reform party, Clan na Poblachta, Mr. Seán MacBride.

Soon Dr. Browne had prepared a scheme for the provision, for mothers — before, during and after childbirth — of free family practitioner care, free specialist, consultant, and hospital treatment if required, free visits from midwives in their own homes, if required, and free dental and optical treatment. Details of Dr. Browne's "revolutionary plan" were published in the *Sunday Independent* in September 1950. There was consternation that Sunday morning as bishops read the story in their palaces. The predictable but devastating response came, after the autumn meeting at Maynooth, in a confidential letter to Mr. Costello from the Bishop of Ferns, Dr. Staunton.

The letter stated: "The powers taken by the State in the proposed Mother and Child Health Service are in direct opposition to the rights of the family and of the individual and are liable to very great abuse. Their character is such that no assurance that they would be used in moderation could justify their enactment. If adopted in law they would constitute a ready-made instrument for future totalitarian aggression.

"The right to provide for the health of children belongs to parents, not to the State. The State has the right to intervene only in a subsidiary capacity, to supplement, not to supplant. •

"It may help indigent or neglected parents; it may not dep-

21

rive 90 per cent of parents of their rights because of 10 per cent necessitous or neglected parents.

"It is not sound social policy to impose a State medical service on the whole community on the pretext of relieving the necessitous 10 per cent from the so called indignity of the means test.

"The right to provide for the physical education of children belongs to the family and not to the State. Experience has shown that physical or health education is closely interwoven with important moral questions on which the Catholic Church has definite teaching.

"Education in regard to motherhood includes instruction in regard to sex relations, chastity and marriage. The State has no competence to give instruction in such matters. We regard with the greatest apprehension the proposal to give to local medical officers the right to tell Catholic girls and women how they should behave in regard to this sphere of conduct at once so delicate and sacred.

"Gynaecological care may be, and in some other countries is, interpreted to include provision for birth limitations and abortion. We have no guarantee that State officials will respect Catholic principles in regard to these matters. Doctors trained in institutions in which we have no confidence may be appointed as medical officers under the proposed services, and may give gynaecological care not in accordance with Catholic principles".

The submissive response of the politicians - and their disowning of Dr. Browne - can be read in Dr. John Whyte's book, *Church and State in Modern Ireland*, which used the correspondence dramatically published by Dr. Browne. In the Dáil Mr. John Costello, the Taoiseach and Fine Gael leader, professed "I am an Irishman second; I am a Catholic first. If the hierarchy give me any direction with regard to Catholic social teaching or Catholic moral teaching, I accept without qualifications in all respects the teaching of the hierarchy and the Church to which I belong".

In a private memorandum Mr. MacBride wrote: "The science of government involves the task of ensuring a harmonious relationship between the Churches and civil government. Every possible effort should be made to avoid the creation of a situation where there is real, or apparent, clash between the Church and the State... It is, of course, impossible for us to ignore the views of the hierarchy. Even if, as Catholics, we are prepared to take the responsibility of disregarding their views, which I do not think we can do, it would be politically impossible to do. We must therefore accept the views of the hierarchy on this matter".

Replying to the letter from Mr. MacBride in which he asked Dr. Browne to resign, Dr. Browne wrote, "your letter is a model of the two-faced hypocrisy and humbug so characteristic of you. Your references to a conflict between the spiritual and temporal authorities will occasion a smile among the many people who remember the earlier version of your kaleidoscopic self".

Commenting on Dr. Browne's resignation *The Irish Times* said "This is a sad day for Ireland. It is not so important that the Mother and Child Scheme has been withdrawn, to be replaced by an alternative project embodying a means test. What matters more is that an honest, far-sighted and energetic man has been driven out of active politics. The most serious revelation, however, is that the Roman Catholic Church would seem to be the effective government of this country".

In *The Bell* magazine the writer Sean Ó Faoláin wrote that the Browne case showed that the Republic had two parliaments, "a parliament at Maynooth and a parliament in Dublin... The Dáil proposes; Maynooth disposes. The Dáil had, when up against the Second Parliament, only one right of decision: the right to surrender".

Following the loss of support from two independents, the divided coalition government was forced into "the pork and barrel" election of May 1951 which was won by Fianna Fáil, whose leader, Mr. de Valera, had remained silent during the Mother and Child debacle. According to Dick Walsh in his book *The Party,* Fianna Fáil's reaction to the humiliation of a potential challenger was smug and cynical; it ignored the damage which the affair inflicted on the south and the opportunity for claims of Rome Rule which it presented to unionists.

But records of the Fianna Fáil government of 1951-54 which are in the State Paper Office show that behind the scenes Mr. de Valera travelled to St. Peter's Presbytery in Drogheda on Friday April 17th 1952 for urgent talks with Cardinal D'Alton. The bishops had threatened to publish their criticisms of a revised Health Bill which had been drafted by the Minister for Health, James Ryan. De Valera succeeded in persuading the Cardinal to use his influence, as chairman of the hierarchy, to avoid publication of the statement. This was done by a Monsignor who phoned the offices of *The Irish Independent* and *The Irish Press* and stopped the publication of the statement in the next morning's papers. (*The Irish Times,* which had so angered the bishops for its stance on the Mother and Child Scheme had not been sent an advance copy of the statement). The price which de Valera paid for this publicity reprieve was to agree to another meeting of an episcopal committee and Government ministers at which the bill was to be further modified to meet the hierarchy's objections.

Mr. de Valera gave an oral report to his cabinet colleagues at the next government meeting. It was a classic instance of what Dr. Keogh calls "informal consensus". While Dr. Whyte lists only sixteen statutes out of 1,800 measures before the Oireachtas between 1923 and 1965, he is aware that account needs to be taken of the interests of bishops in non-statute matters such as education and he suspects that the list of the involvement of the bishops in legislation is probably incomplete.

Dr. Fanning has published details of the subsequent meeting, on April 21st 1953, between the committee of bishops and government ministers at Áras an Uachtaráin, the President's official residence. In a remarkable instance of "the special position" *de facto* of the Catholic bishops, they obtained from the government delegation virtually all the amendments which they sought to the Health Bill of 1953. "Given that the President might be - and, in the event, was - called upon to refer the Health bill to the Supreme Court for a decision on whether its provisions were repugnant to the constitution, it seems extraordinary that the possible constitutional improprieties involved in ministers and bishops coming together to haggle over the wording of legislation under the President's roof seem to have occured to none of the participants", Dr. Fanning writes.

24

"The explanation may be that, 30 years after independence, the coalition between the authorities of Church and State had become so intimate that the choice of meeting-place probably reflects no more than a desire, on the part of ministers, not to have to make their way once more to an archbishop's palace or a presbytery and, on the part of bishops, to an inclination to avoid the publicity and attendant accusations of directly interfering in government business which might attach to their going to Government Buildings".

The government team was led by Mr. de Valera; the hierarchy's delegation consisted of Archbishop Thomas Kinane of Cashel, Bishop Michael Browne of Galway, Bishop Cornelius Lucey of Cork and Bishop Staunton of Ferns. Present were neither Cardinal D'Alton nor the powerful Archbishop of Dublin, Dr. McQuaid, who was on a visit to Australia. To avoid tension, Mr. de Valera opened the talks with a profession of his acceptance of "the position of the bishops as the authoritative teachers of faith and morals". In particular, he endorsed a recent address by Archbishop Kinane asserting the Catholic Church's authority to judge whether "political, social and economic theories are in harmony with God's law".

In his assessment of the secret background to the 1953 Health Act, Dr. Fanning concludes that though it was "a remarkable demonstration of the hierarchy's political musele, Mr de Valera, whose predominance over his cabinet colleagues was undisputed, achieved his aim of avoiding a public denunciation of his government's legislation by the bishops. Insofar as the bill as enacted was a product of consensus politics in Church-State relations and insofar as it was enacted without the kind of public controversy which surrounded the coalition government's Mother and Child scheme in 1951, it could be represented as a political victory rather than a political defeat".

According to confidential British government papers published in 1982 the effect of the Mother and Child Bill controversy set back decisively any slight prospects of north and south reaching a new understanding over partition. In the 1937 constitution, article two laid down "the national territory consists of the whole island of Ireland, its islands and the territorial seas" and article three referred to "the right of the parliament and government established by this constitution to exercise jurisdiction over the whole of that territory". Both these articles enraged northern unionists, already appalled by the Catholic nationalism of its provisions. Only Senator Frank MacDermot, author of a classic book on Wolfe Tone, spoke out against the further obstacles which the constitution was putting in the way of Irish unity. Sean MacEntee, de Valera's Minister for Finance and himself a northerner, said in a *Sunday Times* interview in 1981 that articles two and three would not have been drafted in their present form had de Valera realised that they would alienate the unionists. "If we could have done it again, we would have added 'by free consent of the people', " Mr. MacEntee said. "Nobody dreamed unity could be achieved any other way. We didn't think the addition was necessary". Lord Craigavon, the Prime Minister of Northern Ireland, described the territorial claims as "presumptuous".

In Ottawa on September 7th 1948 Mr. Costello announced the breaking of the Free State's last connection with the Commonwealth and its establishment as a Republic. This was formalised in November with the publication by the government of the Republic of Ireland Bill, which declared that "the state that exists under the 1937 constitution is a republic". This action led to the British Government passing the Ireland Act containing the guarantee to northern unionists of their status in the United Kingdom.

It was against the background of the strains caused by these unilateral moves by Irish leaders that the British Ambassador to the Republic, Sir Gilbert Laithwaite, sent his report to London of the Mother and Child row. His despatch, entitled Review of Affairs, was printed and distributed within the Foreign Office and the Commonwealth Relations Office. His assessment was: "The effect of Mr. MacBride's position has been very damaging. The correspondence was equally embarrassing from the point of view of the Taoiseach, for it left the impression that Mr. Costello's conduct had lacked decision if not candour, and that the members of the coalition government had been allowed to go each of them his own way, with only the slightest cabinet control of general policy.

"But in particular it brought out the dominating position

and authority claimed by, and conceded to, the Roman Catholic hierarchy in southern Ireland in matters of public interest which could be presented as having a moral or social aspect. The deference paid by the Government to the views of the hierarchy has gravely disturbed Protestant, and indeed to some extent Catholic, feeling in the Republic, and the hierarchy's attitude may well supply damaging ammunition to opponents of Catholicism in other countries.

"Since the core of the hierarchical objection was the absence of a means test, there are signs too of a degree of underground criticism of the attitude of the bishops among the poorer classes in this country, which is far from usual.

"Above all, the effect of the incident has been to set back decisively any prospects that there might have been (and these were never more than the slightest) of an understanding between the north and south over partition".

Constitutional Change

Remarkably, however, there was to be a rapprochement between north and south under the leadership of Terence O'Neill and Seán Lemass. In the south economic planning and expansion was directed by the head of the department of finance, T.K. Whitaker, and the protectionist policies of de Valera were abandoned. In 1965 the Anglo-Irish Free Trade Agreement was signed with Britain. The same year Lemass went north to meet O'Neill at Stormont, a meeting, in Richard Rose's words, possessing "all the overtones and anxieties, in Irish terms, of a summit meeting between Russian and American leaders".

The Lemass-O'Neill promise was overtaken by sectarian conflict by the end of the 1960s between the nationalist and unionist communities in Northern Ireland. Craigavon's policy of "a Protestant Parliament for a Protestant people" had been based on callous and deliberate discrimination against the Catholic minority, and a new generation sought civil rights and equality. The public in the south became more aware of the shortcomings of the 1937 constitution as a document suitable for a united Ireland. In accord with the more open-minded approach of the 1960s the Taoiseach, Mr. Lemass, established an all party committee to review the constitution.

Under the chairmanship of Mr. George Colley it presented its report shortly before Christmas 1967. Its three main recommendations were to delete the names of the religious denominations from the constitution, to make provision for divorce for Protestants and to remove article three which claims jurisdiction over all 32 counties by the Republic. But the committee's terms of reference did not commit political parties to implement its recommendations. The report soon gathered dust on the shelves.

The Republic's politicians were aware of two main strands in the debate: the first viewpoint advocated changes in the constitution to reduce fears of undue Catholic influence and thus, hopefully, pave the way for reunification; the second viewpoint maintained that the constitution was outdated, that it bore the marks of Catholicism and that it should be updated to create a pluralist society in the Republic.

Mr. Lemass' successor, Mr. Jack Lynch, set up a new all-party committee in May 1972. Its terms of reference were: "With a view to contributing to a peaceful settlement of the Northern Ireland situation it has been agreed to set up an inter-party committee to establish the common ground between the parties represented on the committee on the constitutional, legal, economic, social and other relevant implications of a united Ireland and to make recommendations as to the steps now required to create conditions conducive to a united Ireland."

The chairman, Mr. Michael O'Kennedy, made it known that the members were dealing with a constitution for the 26 counties. The Fine Gael leader, Mr. Liam Cosgrave, urged the adoption of a new constitution to replace the "divisive" 1937 one which he said should be buried quietly.

Support for a new constitution appropriate for 32 counties was voiced in March 1972 by the leader of the Labour party, Mr. Brendan Corish. At the 1971 Fianna Fáil Ard-Fheis, Mr. Lynch had said he was willing to grasp nettles such as divorce. The general mood seemed to favour overall constitutional review rather than piecemeal changes to the existing constitution. But there was consensus in favour of deletion of the special position of the Catholic Church. Even approval for such a move was forthcoming from the new Cardinal Archbishop of Armagh, Dr. William Conway, who said that he would not weep any tears over its departure. Accordingly, the Lynch government decided to propose the deletion of the two sections of article 44 referring to the special position of the Catholic Church and the recognition of other denominations. It was considered opportune by the government to hold this on December 7th 1972 along with a proposal to reduce the voting age from 21 to 18 years of age.

Such a referendum required the government to pass a bill through both houses of the Oireachtas before putting it before the electorate for a direct vote. Moving the second stage of the Fifth Amendment of the Constitution Bill on Thursday November 2nd, Mr. Lynch said that as it seemed that both sections were divisive and unnecessary, they ought to go. He pointed out that the firm guarantee of religious liberty and freedom of conscience would remain. Mr. Liam Cosgrave pledged Fine Gael's support for the removal of "the special position" which he said should never have been put in, the constitution in the first place by Fianna Fáil.

Mr Frank Cluskey said that the Labour party had sought these deletions for some time. The Labour party, he said, did not think that the constitution should be changed in the context of the Northern Ireland situation but should be changed because as it stood it was wrong. He hoped this change would be a start towards other changes which were needed.

Sceptical that the bill would do much to advance peace between the two communities in the north was Dr. Conor Cruise O'Brien, former diplomat, historian, writer and then a Labour deputy in Dublin North East, a constituency which he shared with Mr. Haughey. But he thought the Bill was too little, too late. In an indirect reference to Harold Wilson's description of the Republic as a theocratic State, Dr. O'Brien suggested that the real reason Mr. Lynch had brought forward this bill was to save himself embarrassment with British statesmen. "What would have happened if Cardinal Conway had said that he would shed tears?" he asked. "He did indicate that he would be opposed to the repeal of Article 41 (2-3) which prohibits divorce", Dr. O'Brien added. "No proposals concerning that are before us now".

Dr. O'Brien said he doubted that Mr. Lynch's government was serious about changing a constitution which was no longer suitable, as for instance in regard to the article banning divorce. This article did not protect the family, merely the government's hypocrisy. It was useless to remove the special position of the Catholic Church article without also removing the article relating to divorce. While supporting the referendum, Dr. O'Brien concluded that it was "a tiny mouse to come out of the mountain of the government's deliberations, and it is utterly inadequate to deal with the horror of the situation in which we are now involved".

More optimistic about the effect of the 1972 referendum on northern opinion was Dr. FitzGerald, who noted the positive welcome from the SDLP and from a former unionist minister, Mr. Roy Bradford: "Those who have hitherto suggested that neither this limited change, nor further more important adjustments to our constitution, to be proposed at a later stage, would be of any interest to opinion in northern Ireland, can now be seen to have been talking nonsense", he said at a Fine Gael meeting.

"It is also significant that there have been few negative reactions to this proposed amendment from Roman Catholic clergy in northern Ireland who are close to the problem. At this point in the evolution of the northern crisis we owe a special duty to the suffering people of the north, and we are bound to do what little we can to help them towards a brighter future".

When the campaign started, Mr. Lynch presented the removal of the "special position" as the first step in the Republic's alignment with the north and as evidence of its willingness to accommodate the views of Protestants.

The Fifth Amendment to the constitution was carried by 84 per cent of those who voted in a low poll which involved only 50.7 per cent of the electorate. In the constituencies within the diocese of Cork and Ross there was only 75 per cent support for Mr. Lynch's call for "a new Ireland", despite the strong popularity of the Taoiseach in his home base. The reason for this below average turnout was the fact that the sturdy old-guard Bishop of Cork and Ross, Dr. Cornelius Lucey, had campaigned against it.

In what was described by commentators as a hollow victory for Mr. Lynch, there was little disguising the fact that half of the electorate cared little about Northern Ireland, and the leader of the fast-expanding Democratic Unionist Party, the Rev. Ian Paisley, was not slow to comment that Mr. Lynch's view of a new Ireland seemed to have met with lack-lustre enthusiasm.

In a perceptive report in the London-based *Catholic Herald*, Donal Mooney observed: "The clamour from the north, it seems, will be furnished only by the Government showing a willingness to take on the Catholic Church on issues - such as contraception, divorce and adoption laws, but possibly not abortion for which there is no great demand in the north - which will not meet with the episcopal neutrality shown in the Article 44 issue. Mr. Lynch has, for the moment at least, denied that he had contemplated moving into such tricky waters. But the clamour from the north may eventually be too much for him. Should he indeed eventually move on that issue he is unlikely to have an easy passage. There is ample evidence to suggest that even the more liberal of the Irish bishops will draw the line at divorce and contraception, not even to mention abortion. And the voters who recently swore to defend article 44 will almost certainly have learned a lesson. Next time out they will make their move earlier and more decisively".

Chapter 2

CONTRACEPTION: ROUND ONE

From the mid 1960s much was written about how the Republic was becoming urbanised, prosperous and independent minded. In the post Vatican II situation the "priest-ridden" image was fading. This mood of national progress was heightened in February 1973 with the election of a Fine Gael-Labour government under Mr. Liam Cosgrave and Mr. Brendan Corish. A sixteen year period of Fianna Fáil rule had ended. Mr. Jack Lynch, who had campaigned mainly on his Northern Ireland policy, lost to an opposition which presented a programme of economic expansion and social reform for the Republic. Soon, however, this government was to be embroiled in the issue of contraception.

It was little noticed during the election that the *Irish Catholic* newspaper urged its readers to write to TDs and Senators in their own area demanding that they should oppose any proposal to facilitate the practice in the Republic of contraception, and that the newspaper reported a good reception to this appeal. The *Irish Catholic* also provided its readers with a specimen letter which they could copy:

"Dear Senator/Deputy, I look to you to oppose both by your vote and your influence the Family Planning Bill which has been given a first reading in the Senate. You have no mandate from me to support this bill or any subsequent bill, having the effect of facilitating the use of contraceptives".

"Pluralism" was a missing word in the election. The politicians wisely steered away from subjects which would provoke the wrath of the Catholic Church; they knew it was not politic to advance ideas and programmes that would not conform to the conservative socio-religious attitudes of the voters. An assessment of Church-State relations, however, has to take account not only of politicians and churchmen but also of judges and women. In the liberalisation of Irish society and public attitudes, the judgements of the Supreme Court and the campaign of the Women's Liberation Movement played an influential part. Using their powers of judicial review, the Supreme Court judges interpreted the constitution in a way which put the emphasis on individual rights and liberties; the women demanded their rights and spurned the domestic hearth role assigned to them by Mr. de Valera.

Despite the loyal acceptance by the hierarchy of Pope Paul VI's condemnation of artificial forms of birth control in his controversial 1968 encyclical, *Humanae Vitae,* there was a growing popular demand in the Republic for the legalisation of contraceptives. Under the 1935 law, the importation, manufacture and sale of contraceptives had been forbidden. Advertising of contraceptives was also forbidden under various accompanying censorship acts. Despite a liberalisation of the censorship laws by Mr. Brian Lenihan in 1967, those relating to contraceptives had not been changed. Such laws, widely accepted in the 1930s onwards, were anomalous by the 1970s. In 1974 doctors were to estimate that 35,000 women were taking the pill on prescription each month for "medical reasons". The law, too, was an obvious difficulty for customs officers. Despite the laws forbidding the sale of contraceptives, the Irish Family Planning Association, a non-profit-making organisation, was providing contraceptives and giving advice to patients about planning of families.

The first attempt to change the law came in 1971 during Mr. Lynch's period as Taoiseach - it came not from the government but from a group of young Senators, Mary Robinson, John Horgan and Trevor West. Their bill caused the government to agree in principle in mid-March that it would change the law on contraceptives.

Soon the pulpits of the archdiocese of Dublin were thundering. On Sunday 28 March priests read out Archbishop McQuaid's warning that if legislation was passed which offended the objective moral law it would be "a curse upon our country". Affirming that the right to contraception was "a right that cannot even exist", Dr. McQuaid explained that the use of a contraceptive by an individual person was a matter of private morality; publicly to make contraceptives available was a matter of public morality. "Given the proneness of

33

our human nature to evil, given the enticement of bodily satis-
faction, given the widespread modern incitement to unchas-
tity, it must be evident that an access hitherto unlawful to contraceptive devices will prove a most certain occasion of sin,
especially to immature persons. The public consequences of
immorality that must follow for the whole society are only too
clearly seen in other countries", he warned.

As Dr. McQuaid's letter was being read by a priest in the
Pro-Cathedral, eight women and a man staged a walk-out.
One of the women shouted to the priest, "This is absolute
rubbish". At an evening Mass in Haddington Road a priest
had just said that "any contraceptive act is wrong in itself"
when a well-known lady journalist, shouted out "this is a
wicked pastoral. It is disgraceful and contrary to *Humanae
Vitae*. This is church dictatorship". A mother of three children, stood up and said "this is a matter that should be
decided by women alone. Why should men dictate to us how
many children we should have? We are leaving this church in
protest".

It was women who staged the most spectacular publicity
stunt against the 1935 law. This was the organised trip on the
"contraceptive train". When the train arrived at Connolly
Station in Dublin from Belfast, the passengers - members of
the Women's Liberation Movement - flaunted their bags full
of contraceptives purchased in the North. In the spotlight of
the television cameras, the women marched through the bar-
riers without their purchases being confiscated by customs
officers. "The law is obsolete", the women shouted.

But where it counted - in the legislative chamber in Leinster
House - nothing was done to change the law by the Lynch government. So hostile was it to actual reform that the government denied the bill of the three senators a first reading.

In the more reformist mood of 1973, Mrs. Robinson
launched a second attempt to change the law. Unlike the 1971
bill, her 1973 bill was given a first reading, that is permission
to publish and circulate the bill. Introducing the bill in early
November Mrs. Robinson proposed that the Minister for
Health should licence the sale of contraceptives in chemist
shops and in hospitals, though some should be available on
prescription only. The innovative feature of the bill, she said,

was that it aimed to take the question of contraception out of the criminal area and place it within welfare.

Before the bill's circulation, support of ministers and deputies had been canvassed. A more moderate bill than the 1971 version might embarrass the government and force its hand, Mrs. Robinson said. Response from deputies and senators was low-key but positive. Nor did she anticipate opposition from the churches. "There may be individual churchmen who will oppose it", she said in *The Catholic Standard,* "But I feel that the hierarchy as a whole would do little to block the new bill".

But on Sunday 26 November 1973 the hierarchy entered the contraceptive debate with the publication of a major statement on the principles which it felt should govern Church-State relations. This statement was an enormous advance from the response made two years earlier by Archbishop McQuaid. It recognised that it was not a matter for the Irish bishops to decide whether the law should be changed or not but that this was the responsibility of legislators. It was the clear teaching of the Catholic Church, the statement added, that the use of contraceptives was morally wrong and that no change in State law could change that situation. But it did not follow that the State was bound to prohibit the sale and the importation of contraceptives. The real question facing legislators was what effect would the increased availability of contraceptives have on the quality of life in the Republic. What the legislators had to decide was whether, on balance, a change in the law would do more harm than good, by damaging the character of the society for which they were responsible. That was a question of public, not private, morality.

In *The Irish Times* James Downey reported that the statement was taken calmly by Dáil and Senate supporters of Mrs. Robinson's bill but that in some government - especially Labour - circles the reaction was furious. "The statement was denounced by highly placed persons in extraordinarily strong language," Mr. Downey added. "Among the words used were 'dishonesty', 'irresponsibility', and 'amazing political insensitivity'." Much of the astonishment in Leinster House related to the timing of the statement's publication. It was

35

issued at a critical juncture when the Sunningdale agreement was within reach on the formation of a power-sharing executive involving the Ulster unionists, the Social Democratic and Labour Party and the Alliance Party, and the Dublin government hoped that this settlement would lead to the setting up of an effective all-Ireland institution. Mr. Downey quoted an influential politician as saying, "what is at stake is building confidence within Northern Ireland and between north and south, and what could be more calculated to destroy that than the appearance of Church domination in the Republic?"

A few weeks later the Supreme Court gave a new direction to the debate when it delivered its now famous McGee judgement. This case concerned a mother of four children, Mrs. Mary McGee, who lived in a mobile home near Skerries, County Dublin. For the sake of her health she had been advised by a doctor that she should not have any more children. She was fitted with a diaphragm which was to be used along with spermicidal jelly, a small supply of which was given to her by a doctor. When that supply was finished, she sent for a further supply by post from England. That package was intercepted and seized by customs officers, acting under the powers conferred by the 1935 Act. Mrs. McGee sought a declaration in the High Court that section 17 of the law was unconstitutional. This was rejected by Mr. Justice Ó Caoimh. Mrs. McGee appealed to the Supreme Court which ruled that those parts of the law which forbade citizens to import contraceptives for personal use were unconstitutional.

The central component in the Supreme Court judgement was the decision that family planning rested with the couple alone, and that the couple's right to make an unimpeded decision was protected by the constitution. This declaration opened the way for a revision of the position of women in Irish society.

On 21 February 1974 Mrs. Robinson's bill reached the second stage in the Senate, where the Minister for Justice, Mr. Patrick Cooney, announced the government's intention to publish its own bill within a fortnight. Mr. Cooney said that the rationale of the McGee judgement was that married couples had the right to have access to contraceptives which was denied to them under the existing law. This limitation to a married couple was described by Mr. West as ridiculous and impossible, and by Mrs. Robinson as constitutionally impossible and legally indefensible.

On 27 March 1974 the government's Control on Importation, Sale and Manufacture of Contraceptives Bill proposed that contraceptives could be imported and sold under licence by chemists; only married couples were to have access to contraceptives; widows and widowers were regarded as unmarried since the bill defined such a person as one "who has no living spouse"; fines of up to £500 or a year in prison - or both - would follow convictions before a higher court. Summary convictions for manufacturing, importing or selling abortifacients could lead to a fine of £100 or six months imprisonment.

Senator Robinson, whose bill had been defeated by 32 votes to 10 in the Senate the previous day, said the government bill "will to some extent make us the laughing stock of Europe in its present form". But she accepted that the proposed legislation would give respectability to people already using contraceptives who at the moment did so with "the aura of criminals".

Sensationally, however, the government's bill was defeated by a margin of 75 to 61 on 16 July when the Taoiseach, Liam Cosgrave, led six Fine Gael deputies into the opposition lobby. To the horror and amazement of ministers such as Garret FitzGerald, Conor Cruise O'Brien and Justin Keating, Mr. Cosgrave was accompanied by the Minister for Education, Mr. Dick Burke, and by backbenchers, Mr. Oliver J Flanagan, Mr. Tom Enright, Mr. Des Governey, Mr. Martin Finn and Mr. Joe McLoughlin. In his Dáil sketch *Irish Times* commentator John Healy wrote that "the most forceful speech on the three-day contraceptive debate was made by the man who never opened his mouth but talked with his feet - Liam Cosgrave".

With the defeat of the bill nothing was done until 1979 when the Minister for Health in Mr. Lynch's third administration, Mr. Charles Haughey, presented his "Irish solution for an Irish problem" which was criticised as sectarian by Dr. FitzGerald. Mr. Haughey's Health (Family Planning) Act, 1979, was regarded by many lawyers as being probably unconstitutional because, while the Supreme Court had declared firmly in the McGee case that the family planning decision rested solely with the couple, the bill made the decision dependent on a doctor being satisfied that the application for a prescription for contraceptives was for 'bona fide' family planning purposes.

In the Dáil, Mr. Haughey said he had not regarded it necessary that "we should conform to the position obtaining in any other country". It was a reasonable attempt to meet the difficulties of a complicated situation and to reconcile some passionately held conflicting views in the community. He predicted that it would accord with the wishes of the overwhelming majority of sensible people in the country and that for the first time it would provide a comprehensive family planning service for all the people.

Mr. Haughey's legislation was the product of consultations with the churches, particularly the Catholic Church. Unlike the days of de Valera when politicians came to churchmen, the Catholic episcopal delegation came to Mr. Haughey at the Customs House. As in the 1952-3 consultations with Mr. de Valera on a Health Act, the bishops in their consultations with Mr. Haughey obtained acceptance of much of their submission, not least the Act's recognition of natural methods of regulating births. The bishops welcomed the controls and limitations on the distribution of contraceptives and warned legislators, doctors and pharmacists of their "grave responsiblity" to ensure that the Act was not operated in a way which would make contraceptives more and more freely available with the passage of time.

The Catholic bishops also stressed that State legislation did not alter the fact that in God's design contraceptive intercourse was morally wrong. But there was no opposition to the Haughey measure. During the passage of the bill, the Bishop of Kerry, Dr. Kevin McNamara, wrote in *Doctrine and Life* that "it is not the State's duty to make better Christians, still less better Catholics".

The bill did not correspond to the belief of the Protestant Churches that married couples had the right to make decisions for themselves in the personal matter of birth control and that natural planning methods are not necessarily morally superior to contraceptive devices. The Methodists, for instance, complained that Mr. Haughey had not accepted their recommendation that all health boards should provide a comprehensive family planning service. The Methodist Church's Council for Social Welfare rejected "the whole idea of doctors and pharmacists being set up as moral arbiters in control of contraceptives, including non-medical items".

A former cabinet colleague said that at that time Mr. Haughey was the only minister with the courage and pragmatism to introduce a family planning act. But his measure was closer to the wishes of the Catholic bishops than to the Protestant Churches. In seeking a compromise between conflicting views, Mr. Haughey had come down on the side of the Catholic majority. This decision was to hover over him when as Taoiseach in 1980 he assured Northern unionists that everything would be negotiable in a united Ireland.

As far back as 1963 Mr. Haughey had proposed the motion that "minorities have nothing to fear in a United Ireland" at a meeting at Queen's University Belfast. In his address Mr. Haughey argued that the 1937 constitution provided "for the fullest possible measure of democracy throughout the entire political process; our minority groups play their full part in our political life and there has never been the slightest whisper of complaint from any quarter in this regard".

Mr. Haughey referred to the general attitude in the Republic, "our outlook, the climate of opinion, our sense of fair play, our public pride in the fact that we have succeeded in building a society free of religious persecution and intolerance. What is really important is not that there couldn't be; there is no longer any argument about it; it is one of the facts of our communal life. It is this outlook and state of mind which, in my opinion, is the greatest possible guarantee that minority and majority could live side by side in peace and harmony in a united Ireland".

Chapter 3

GARRET AND THE VATICAN

Garret FitzGerald's constitutional crusade to remove sectarian features from the Republic's laws and institutions did not begin in October 1981 in a radio station in Donnybrook. As a writer he had expressed his ideas in a seminal article in *Studies* as far back as 1964, and in 1972 he embarked on private initiatives at the Vatican which until now have not been made known to the public. Dr FitzGerald's secret diplomacy involved him in contacts with Pope Paul VI and with two senior prelates of the Roman Curia, Archbishops Giovanni and Benelli and Agostino Casaroli. At these consultations Dr FitzGerald sought to persuade the head of the world's 738 million Roman Catholics of the urgent need for acceptance by the Irish Catholic Church of a non-sectarian pluralist society, north and south of the border.

The progeny of a mixed marriage, Garret FitzGerald was born with a mission to reconcile the "Ulster Scots" and the Gaelic traditions. His mother Mabel, born in Belfast, the daughter of a Presbyterian businessman, was attracted to Irish nationalism and to the poet-revolutionary, Desmond FitzGerald. Both parents fought in the Easter Rising of 1916 and were present in the General Post Office when Pádraig Pearse acknowledged the hopelessness of the situation for the rebels. His father was arrested and sentenced to life imprisonment for his role in the rising but this was commuted twenty years. After being imprisoned in Maidstone and Dartmoor, he was released in 1917. Desmond assisted Michael Collins in London during the Treaty negotiations as Minister for Propaganda, assuming the awesome task of bringing the text of the Treaty to the Mansion House on December 6th 1921. Later he became the Free State's first Minister for External Relations. Thus, Garret FitzGerald's republican credentials are impeccable. So, too, is his deep attachment to his Roman Catholic faith.

This personal inheritance made it impossible for him to accept the theory that there are two separate nations in Ireland. Nor did he accept the theory that Ireland is one nation with a single neo-Gaelic, Roman Catholic culture, into which Northern unionists should return.

For Garret FitzGerald, politics in the south and in the north took wrong turnings after 1920. It has only been since the 1960s that - partly thanks to Vatican II - rigid attitudes began to thaw. In 1964, shortly before he entered politics and five years before the Northern Ireland problem was to become manifest again, Dr FitzGerald published in *Studies* his vision of the new Ireland which needed to be built. The article, appropriately was entitled "Towards a national purpose".

He wrote then of a society which would be the product of the combined Christian, liberal and socialist traditions. "This society would be specifically Irish in its inspiration, proud of its origins and determined that the culture and way of life of Ireland should have a high reputation in the world. This Irish society would draw on the mixed origins of our society - Gaelic, Anglo-Irish, Ulster-Scots and English - and would be neither exclusive nor sectional. It would glory in our mixed inheritance, despising none of it, and elevating no part to a position of pre-eminence over the rest.

In such a society narrowness and intolerance would be regarded as vices meriting social disapproval. Bigotry in any form would not be tolerated; sectarian organisations dedicated to promoting the personal temporal advancement of members of a particular religion would be universally frowned upon.

"Relations between north and south would be based on whole-hearted accpetance of the principle that political unity must be preceded by a unity of hearts ..."

When he wrote the 1972 book, Dr FitzGerald was a rising star in the main opposition party, Fine Gael; he was well known for his contributions, verbal and written, on a range of economic, religious and political issues; in particular, he was acknowledged as an expert on the European Economic Community, of which Ireland was to become a member, along with Britain, on January 1st, 1973. In the book he presented the case for a federal arrangement between north and south.

He also listed "the steps which might usefully be taken in the Republic at this stage as an earnest wish of its people to seek a reunification of the country in terms that could be acceptable to northern Protestants".

These were: the repeal by referendum of the constitutional provisions on the special position of the Catholic Church and divorce; amendment of the law banning the import and sale of contraceptives; a modification of the system dealing with obscene printed matter, substituting a new version of the older system of control by prosecution for the existing censorship system, and the removal of the Irish language requirements in examinations and in recruitments for, and promotion within, the public service.

In a passage which has echoes of the future New Ireland Forum, Dr FitzGerald wrote: "The Irish problem is quite simply the fruit of northern Protestant reluctance to become part of what they regard as an authoritarian southern Catholic State. This is the obstacle to be overcome. It is *their* fears that have to be resolved if tensions in the norh are to be eased, and Ireland is to be united. It is true that this will pose problems for the Catholic majority in the Republic - problems of adjustment to a pluralist society - but this is a second, and hopefully, less difficult stage in the affair, and one that in any event cannot be successfully tackled until the precise nature of Protestant fears is understood".

Within months Dr FitzGerald, the intellectual, was in a position of power as Minister for Foreign Affairs in the Fine Gael-Labour government headed by Mr Liam Cosgrave, the son of W.T. Cosgrave, who had established a stable democracy in the first ten difficult years of the Irish State before ceding power in 1932 to Eamon de Valera. The new government, described by Raymond Smith as the team of all talents, took office at an important juncture in Ireland's formulation of policy towards Northern Ireland and only months after joining the EEC. As Foreign Minister, Dr FitzGerald was in place to exert a major influence on two of his prime preoccupations. Within days he was in contact with Prime Minister, Edward Heath, and Foreign Minister, Sir Alec Douglas Home, about the Dublin government's views on the direction Anglo-Irish talks should take. Within weeks he had outraged the Rev Ian

Paisley by visiting Catholics and Protestants in Belfast. Attendance at an EEC Council of Ministers at which aid for North Vietnam was high on the agenda convinced him of the need for an expansion of Ireland's foreign service to match its new global responsibilities as an EEC member State. In July he met the veteran Soviet Foreign Minister, Mr Andrei Gromyko, in Helsinki, where they buried Catholic Ireland's traditional hostility to Red Russia and advanced arrangements for opening diplomatic relations which would lead to the establishment of embassies in Dublin and Moscow. In Helsinki, where he was attending the Conference on Security and Cooperation in Europe, Dr FitzGerald advocated the creation of a new Europe, which would reverse its past colonial stance towards the Third World and which would unite nations in mutual respect for diverse social and economic systems, with a diminishing need for military alliances.

Impressed by the idealism and intellectual vigour of the Irish newcomer to the international diplomatic scene was a slender, bespectacled diplomat, Agostino Casaroli, the head since 1967 of the Holy See's Council for Public Affairs. In effect, Archbishop Casaroli was the foreign minister of the Holy See. While the young Irishman was only beginning to make his name, Archbishop Casaroli's reputation was already well established.

He was styled by Italian journalists as "the Henry Kissinger of the Vatican". In 1961, Pope John XXIII, the pontiff who convened the Council to renew Catholicism and sent peace signals rather than denunciations to the Soviet leader, Nikita Krushchev, assigned Casaroli to Vienna as head of the Vatican delegation to a conference on diplomatic relations. In February 1971 Archbishop Casaroli went to Moscow to sign the treaty on the Non-proliferation of Nuclear Weapons. Archbishop Casaroli had become the principal architect of Pope Paul VI's policy of *Ostpolitik,* the improvement of the conditions of life for Catholics living behind "the Iron Curtain" and the promotion of peace and debate between the west and communism. The Archbishop's attendance in Helsinki at the conference on European Security was the first time the Holy See was represented at an international conference since Cardinal Consalvi's presence at the 1815 Congress of Vienna, which remapped Europe after the fall of Napoleon.

The Archbishop not only directed the Vatican's *Ostpolitik* but he also presided over the operation of the Vatican's diplomatic service, consisting then of 36 nuncios, 36 pronuncios, 16 apostolic delegates and one chargé d'affairs. According to the late Archbishop Igno Cardinale, the aim of Vatican diplomacy is "the art and science of fostering good relations between Church and State".

It had been in 1930 that the government of W.T. Cosgrave established diplomatic relations with the Holy See. During the arrangements for the appointment of Archbishop Paschal Robinson, a Franciscan, the Vatican decided that the Red Hat should go to Archbishop MacRory of Armagh rather than to Archbishop Byrne of Dublin, as advocated by Mr Cosgrave. According to historian, Dr Dermot Keogh, Archbishop Robinson was "both liked and respected by politicians and ecclesiastics alike. His presence helped indirectly the smooth running of Church-State relations. The Vatican also received the mosts incisive reports from Ireland, which made it unlikely that misunderstandings could arise between Rome and Ireland either on the secular or the sacred plane for as long as Robinson was nuncio to Dublin".

Since 1969 the nuncio to Ireland was Dr Gaetano Alibrandi, a Sicilian, a controversial figure whose relations with both government and hierarchy were at best cool. By dealing directly with Cardinal Casaroli, Dr FitzGerald was bypassing the head of the nunciature in Dublin.

"The essence of a Vatican statesman" is how Archbishop Casaroli is described by an American priest, F X Murphy, who gives a vivid portrait of the prelate in a book, *The Papacy Today:* "Known to colleagues as the artisan of concordats, Casaroli is an affable conversationalist, astute and witty, whose knowledge of the church structure and its relations with the outside world is unequalled in the present generation".

Nor had Ireland had a Foreign Minister like Garret FitzGerald, a lay Catholic inspired by the fresh approach of Pope John XXIII. In his first months as Foreign Minister he had begun pursuing his Northern Ireland and European

44

objectives. Here in Helsinki the opportunity arose for him to present to the Vatican's senior diplomat the case for acceptance of a non-sectarian, pluralist Ireland.

Dr FitzGerald's consultations with Archbishop Casaroli in Helsinki - and the subsequent sequels in the Vatican in September 1973 and March 1977 - were never reported in the media. The full details will not be disclosed until the Vatican opens its archives at some distant future date; or if either Dr FitzGerald writes his autobiography once he leaves active politics or in due course when the records of the Department of Foreign Affairs become available to historians. For the first time, however, the story of these important developments in the relations between the Holy See and the Irish State can be told in outline - and general conclusions can be drawn.

In Helsinki Archbishop Casaroli and Dr FitzGerald had informal talks during which the situation in Northern Ireland loomed high in their concerns and during which the Irishman explained to the Italian his belief in the need for the creation of a pluralist State in the Republic. What struck the shrewd Vatican diplomat was that Dr FitzGerald's concept of pluralism was rooted in Christian fellowship, not on a secular anti-clericalism. Archbishop Casaroli was also stimulated by the different perspective on developments north and south given by Dr FitzGerald compared with the reports he had read from the Irish Bishops and from the nuncio. He was attracted to FitzGerald's *Nordpolitik*.

Archbishop Casaroli listened closely to Dr FitzGerald's argument that the northern Protestants realised that in a united Ireland there would still be a 75 per cent Catholic majority and that they feared the loss of their civil liberies in regard to matters such as contraception and divorce, liberties which had been removed by the Irish State in the 1920s and 1930s from the minority Protestant community in the south. He was also interested in Dr FitzGerald's presentation of a religious dimension in the conflict, particularly in the way mixed marriages policy and separate schooling kept the unionist and nationalist communities apart and perpetuated fears and suspicions of each other. Dr FitzGerald made noteworthy use of a 1968 study by Professor Richard Rose which had shown that 62 per cent of Catholics in Northern Ireland favoured mixing Catholics and Protestants together in State schools. Only 28 per cent disapproved and 10 per cent had no opinion.

The education question was of direct concern to Archbishop Casaroli, because in the diocese of Down and Connor (which includes Belfast) a dispute was growing between Bishop William Philbin and a group of Catholic parents about the conferring of confirmation on some Catholic children attending State schools.

The Helsinki talks were obviously considered worthwhile by Dr FitzGerald, who on his return to Dublin wrote formally to Archbishop Casaroli. In advance of a visit to the Vatican which was being arranged through diplomatic channels, Dr FitzGerald in August prepared an *aide memoir* covering the points of the Helsinki conversation on mixed marriages, contraception, divorce and the situation in Northern Ireland. This document was sent as top secret to Cardinal Casaroli through the Irish Embassy to the Holy See. A copy of it was sent by Dr FitzGerald to the Taoiseach, Mr Cosgrave, who made no comment, favourable or critical. Thus, by default, Dr FitzGerald's personal initiative had government support. Members of that government, however, do not recall being briefed on this initiative. It is most unlikely that it was discussed in cabinet.

The opportunity for an early follow-up meeting between Archbishop Casaroli and Dr FitzGerald came in September. In the first flush of Ireland's membership of the European Community Dr FitzGerald had summoned all Ireland's ambassadors back to Iveagh House for a think-in on the nation's foreign policy. An immediate challenge facing Dr FitzGerald was of how to convince the other eight EEC member states of the importance for Ireland, the poorest member state, of a dynamic regional policy. To press Ireland's case for a large regional fund, Dr FitzGerald adopted the Kissinger-style of shuttle diplomacy and arranged for a tour of EEC capitals. While in Rome for talks at the Italian Foreign Ministry, he crossed the Tiber unnoticed and unreported on September 12th for his second encounter - but his first official meeting with the Pope's foreign minister.

In diplomatic exchanges there is the combination of **the**

prepared documentation and the actual selective discussion of the principals. The record of the occasion indicates that Dr FitzGerald explained the situation in Ireland, north and south, and the reasons why - but not imminently - the issues of contraception and divorce would have to be examined in the circumstances of a pluralist society. He also explained that on an island where there was a Protestant majority in the north the Irish government would have to look for some measure of harmonisation in laws and certainly would have to remove wide disparities in law, which could be a source of division.

Dr FitzGerald gave particular emphasis to the problem of mixed marriages, a matter of ecclesiastical rather than State law. He argued that the ban on mixed marriages was in part responsible for the decline in the Protestant population in the south - and which had been misinterpreted in the north by people as being discrimination against Protestants. Catholic Church mixed marriage regulations were a source of tension in Northern Ireland and were used as an argument by those wishing to exacerbate feelings against Catholics in Northern Ireland, ultimately putting Catholics at risk. There was a special dimension to the mixed marriage situation which did not exist anywhere else and which would justify it being looked at in the special Irish situation.

Through the diplomatic channels of the Catholic Church's own bureaucracy - and through his personal contacts inside the Vatican - Cardinal William Conway learned of the Foreign Minister's *démarche,* and pondered the implications of this move for the Irish Catholic Church's strategy to meet the changing circumstances. In September 1963 he had replaced the late Cardinal D'Alton as Archbishop of Armagh, the historic seat of St Patrick, and Primate of All Ireland. In contrast to McQuaid, the Archbishop of Dublin and Primate of Ireland, who told his people that nothing in Vatican II would disturb the tranquillity of their lives, Cardinal Conway noted "a certain sense of spring in the air through the Church as a whole and, if I mistake not, in Ireland also". The Cardinal energetically expanded the re-organisation of the episcopal conference and set up expert commissions to deal with a range of subjects. He also promoted liturgical, architectural and catechetical changes.

It was the misfortune of Cardinal Conway to preside over the Irish Catholic Church at one of its most transitional and turbulent periods in history. He had difficulty in coming to terms with two main challenges of the age: the sectarian violence which erupted in Northern Ireland in 1969 and the coming of secularisation of society in the Republic. In the heady days of the late 1960s the Irish discovered not only that the Catholic Church was not "the perfect society" as portrayed in the penny catechism, but that the post-1922 societies north and south were also far from perfect. The traditional episcopal controls were weakening. In 1970 the bishops agreed to the lifting of the ban forbidding Catholics to study at Dublin's Trinity College without special permission from the Archbishop of Dublin. In 1972 Cardinal Conway shed no tears over the deletion from the constitution of the Catholic Church's "special position".

But as Desmond Fisher argued, in a Thomas Davis lecture, Cardinal Conway had worked out a campaign which aimed "to capture and control the forces of change so that they could be packaged and rationed out as the bishops determined". The Cardinal's influence was detectable in the March 1971 hierarchy statement in response to Mrs Robinson's family planning bill. Whereas Dr McQuaid had denounced it, the bishops appealed to the people not to allow the politicians to introduce "the permissive society" into Ireland.

Referring to abortion, contraception and divorce, the bishops said: "These questions involve issues of grave import for society as a whole, which go beyond purely private morality or private religious belief. Civil law on these matters should respect the wishes of the people who elected the legislators and the bishops confidently hope that the legislators themselves will respect this important principle".

Cardinal Conway, a Belfastman, saw the Northern Ireland conflict in terms of ending decades of Protestant discrimination against Catholics. That discrimination had been exerted for the political and social supremacy of the unionist community. He rejected any suggestion that there was a religious or sectarian element in the conflict. Faced with the demands for integrated education, the Cardinal in 1970 issued a pamphlet defending *Catholic Schools*. He rejected the claim that

Catholic schools were a cause of division in the Northern Ireland community. For the parents - or for the church authorities - to place in jeopardy the gift of communicating the Catholic faith in Catholic schools would be to take on a grave responsibility.

Cardinal Conway was not impressed by the argument that accommodations would have to be made with unionists on issues of sexual morality. For him the question of a united Ireland was something for a distant future. What concerned him was the situation now. He did not believe that the attitudes of the average unionist would be changed in the slightest degree if laws in the Republic were changed. In 1972 he reacted unsympathetically to a report of a working party of the Irish Theological Association proposing the removel of the divorce ban from the constitution. When he appeared in Dublin at a private session of the Oireachtas second all party committee on the constitution he was annoyed at the question put to him - by Garret FitzGerald, incidentally - as to why a law banning the sale of contraceptives was morally essential in one part of the archdiocese of Armagh while its absence on the Northern Ireland side of the diocese was not the subject for the Cardinal's similar attention.

By 1973 Cardinal Conway's leadership of the hierarchy was uncontested. Although an influential figure, the new Archbishop of Dublin, Dr Dermot Ryan, was in the shadow of Armagh. The combination of Dr FitzGerald's consultations in Rome and Mrs Robinson's renewed efforts to legalise contraception made it urgent for the Cardinal to define the hierarchy's response to the pluralist society. It was against this background that the November 1973 guide-lines - the legislators legislate, the bishops preach - were drafted. It was with jubilation - and a sense of relief - that Cardinal Conway finalised a draft text which was a development on the 1971 statement. His main difficulty had been to get the acceptance of the text by the late Bishop of Ossory, Dr Peter Birch, a liberal who doubted the need for church teaching to be supported in law.

The new guide-lines were presented as proof of the Catholic Church's non-interference in politics, but their careful construction scarcely masked the message to the politicians that the bishops would directly appeal to the people - the constituents - on specific issues.

The counter-offensive was based on the domino theory principle that if parliament legalised contraception, society would be asked to accept divorce in a referendum and that abortion and euthanasia would follow. In 1975 the bishops issued a four-part pastoral letter, *Human Life is Sacred,* the manifesto of the counter offensive and using modern media techniques to sell the traditional moral values. It was designed to make it more difficult for the politicians to go ahead with any thoughts of legalising contraception or divorce. The bishops had sensed the change in direction of the tide since the failure of the Coalition's Contraception Bill in July 1974. 1975 was the Holy Year, the Rosary came back into fashion and Oliver Plunkett was canonised a saint.

Another important theme in the early 1970s was the growing readiness of the minority Protestant community in the Republic to voice its support for the adoption by the Oireachtas of family planning legislation and for removing the constitutional ban on divorce. The Church of Ireland Dean of St Patrick's, Victor Griffin, was particularly outspoken in his advocacy of a pluralist society. But both the politicians and the Catholic Church leaders were deaf to the appeals.

In the face of mounting criticism in the media of the ineffective role of the Churches in reducing sectarian tensions in Northern Ireland, Cardinal Conway had seized the initiative by convening the first ever summit meeting of Irish Catholic and Protestant church leaders. This took place at Ballymascanlon, Co Louth, close to the border, in September 1973, coincidentally the month in which Dr FitzGerald was pursuing his diplomatic dialogue with the Vatican. Again, Cardinal Conway exerted his considerable powers of persuasion to ensure that such issues such as mixed marriages and integrated education were not on the agenda - let alone be negotiable. At the second session in 1974 when the power-sharing executive, set up by the Sunningdale Agreement and involving unionists and the SDLP, had presented proposals the evening before on shared schooling in Northern Ireland, Cardinal Conway next morning told the Protestant leaders that this was not to be discussed. Meekly, they obeyed.

Despite the lack of progress towards pluralism, in early 1976 a debate on Church-State relations was conducted publicly by the Minister for Posts and Telegraphs, Dr Conor Cruise O'Brien, and Bishop Jeremiah Newman of Limerick. Dr O'Brien questioned the wisdom of the government, of which he was a minister, in denying to young people "effective means of limiting families and the knowledge of how to limit them". He also described the defeat of the family planning bill in the Dáil in July 1974 as being "a setback to progress towards non-sectarianism". He defined the secular state as one which takes into account "the views of all the citizens, whether they adhere to a religion whose members are in a majority, or to religions whose members are in a minority, that the State should not override one set of opinions by enforcing another set, and in fact that the State should protect equally the rights of people of all religions and those professing no religion".

Dr Newman, who had recently been promoted to the Limerick bishopric from Maynooth College where he had risen to be its President, described Dr O'Brien as "a self-declared agnostic". He rejected Dr O'Brien's charge of sectarianism and he expressed total opposition to a secular society. A secular state "is something we will have to fight against to the end", the bishop said. "It is a challenge to the Church in this country at the moment. We have got to give leadership to the people to stand up against a secular state and those who represent it".

In an address to his Dublin south east constituency on April 28th, Dr FitzGerald intervened in the debate, to present the case for pluralism. In setting out the principles for Church-State relations, Dr FitzGerald illustrated his thesis with reference to the specific issues of schooling, contraception, divorce and abortion. His contribution was described by Professor Enda McDonagh of Maynooth College as "of a kind, if not on a topic, more likely to emanate from a Roy Jenkins or Anthony Crossland". Attention, however, focussed not so much on the principles which Dr FitzGerald enunciated but more on the specifics, a mistake which was to be repeated

51

nearly a decade later when Margaret Thatcher dismissed the three options of the New Ireland Forum while embarking on the serious negotiations which led to the Hillsborough Agreement in November 1985.

When asked by the leader of the Opposition, Mr Lynch, if the government planned to pursue the issue raised by Dr FitzGerald, Mr Cosgrave gave a blunt 'no'; Garret was on his own. Mr Cosgrave left the Dáil in no doubt that he had no plans to promote the pluralist agenda. On moral issues, like his father W T Cosgrave, he took his values from Rome; but like de Valera, on issues of law and order, or political matters, he was capable of defying Rome, as he did in 1975 in a curt dismissal of a private complaint from the Holy See about conditions in Portlaoise Prison.

The FitzGerald-O'Brien contributions, however, elicited an important response from the bishops who issued a statement confirming and clarifying the 1973 guidelines. It was felt by the bishops that Dr Newman might have been overzealous in his insistence of the need for the State to enforce Catholic values. The bishops therefore emphasised that it was not their view that in the law of the state "the principles peculiar to our faith should be made binding on people who do not adhere to that faith", as claimed by Dr O'Brien. They repeated that the main question for legislators was the impact on society of any proposed change in the law.

Dr FitzGerald had been acutely embarrassed by Mr Cosgrave's opposition to the government's own bill on contraception and his hopes of advancing towards pluralism were frustrated domestically by the dogged resistance of the Taoiseach and other members of the cabinet such as Dick Burke, Tom O'Donnell and Mark Clinton. However, as Minister for Foreign Affairs, Dr FitzGerald realised the importance of Ireland's embassy to the Holy See as a medium for explaining government policy and trends in Irish society.

By now seasoned in the world of diplomacy, Dr FitzGerald had come to attach high importance to the Irish Embassy to the Holy See and would not hear of any suggestion that in cost-cutting operations it should be closed. Through the work of Irish diplomats the government had a channel for explaining the importance which it attached to the promotion of reconciliation between the two communities in Northern Ireland; of the need to respect the identities and traditions of both, and of the vulnerability of about 200,000 Catholics living in the strongly Protestant counties of Antrim and Down. In the Republic the government was responding in a calm and moderate way to social changes and to the changing mores of young people. The changes in Italy, Spain and Portugal could be referred to.

The Vatican perception of Ireland was not uniform. There were those who took an idealised view of Ireland, as if it were frozen in time. Just as some Irish Americans had romantic notions of Irish unity, so too inside the Vatican there were officials who had an outdated picture of Ireland as part of Rome's spiritual empire. Others were more in touch with the social realities of modern Ireland and sensitive to the problems which change posed for the Church.

The opportunity for arranging the meeting with Pope Paul VI was provided by the decision of the EEC Heads of Government and their Foreign Ministers to hold their spring summit meeting in Rome on Friday 25th March 1977 to celebrate the twentieth anniversary of the signing of the Treaty of Rome, the Community's constitution. No one knew of Dr FitzGerald's rendezvous in the Vatican.

For a Catholic, particularly an Irish Catholic, the Vatican instils deep emotions. It was to Rome that Daniel O'Connell was travelling when he died in Genoa en route. It was to Rome that de Valera had turned for approval of his constitution and in the papal summer residence of Castel Gandolfo in October 1957, Pius XII had told him that "your constitution is intended to be an instrument of 'Prudence, Justice and Charity' at the service of a community which has never, through its long Christian history, had any doubt about the eternal, as well as the temporal implications of that common good, which it professes to seek through the conjoined prayer, toil and often times heroic sacrifice of its children".

The contrast could not have been greater when, 20 years later, Dr FitzGerald walked into the Apostolic Palace for three appointments in succession - with Pope Paul VI, with Archbishop Benelli and lastly with Archbishop Casaroli. Vatican officials had mixed feelings towards Dr FitzGerald: a certain suspicion of him as an amateur theologian and as an high-powered intellectual who did not possess the simple faith and the obsequious deference to clergy which characterise the outlook of so many Irish Catholic politicians; a regard for his courage and strength of character as he displayed a mastery of his prepared brief and delivered an eloquent presentation of his case.

Pope Paul VI, who was to celebrate his 80th birthday in September 1977, was suffering from arthritis but was still mentally active. He knew that he was reaching the end of a long and troubled pontificate. Succeeding John XXIII, Paul had brought the Second Vatican Council to fruition, had undertaken the difficult task of its implementation and had begun the era of papal travel. "Troubling Pope Paul were genuine worries about the faith and religious consciousness, a reflection of the rigid theological training of his youth and his early priesthood", writes F X Murphy, "Only peripherally involved in the theological stirrings after the end of World War II, he was ill prepared for the radical thinking behind many of the substantial changes in the Church's traditional teaching on religious liberty, on marriage, and on the nature of divine revelation to become conciliar doctrine. Though he promulgated the documents, he was easily persuaded by the fearful cardinals and conservative theologians in his entourage to declare a holding-off of their implementation until the Roman curial offices could give these conditions and decrees an official and restraining interpretation".

In Paul's eyes Cardinal Conway was the archetypal loyal prelate. He was grateful for the support of the Irish bishops in 1968 when he issued *Humanae Vitae,* the controversial papal encyclical condemning artificial forms of birth control. His contact with Ireland stretched back to 1937. He was the *sostituto* or substitute to the then Secretary of State and future Pius XII, Cardinal Pacelli and was familiar with de Valera's lobbying for Vatican support of his constitution. He had also visited Drogheda in the 1950s to see the remains of Oliver Plunkett, whom he canonised at a Mass in the wind-swept St Peter's Square in the autumn of 1975.

Since the outbreak of violence in Northern Ireland he had repeatedly appealed for an end to violence. During the 1971

Synod of Bishops he had a half hour meeting with Cardinal Conway at which he thanked him for the Irish bishops' efforts to restore peace. In a world where he increasingly feared that schism threatened the unity of Catholicism - Hans Kung and the progressives on the left and Archbishop Lefebvre on the right - he had a special attachment to Ireland as a traditional Catholic country. His English-speaking secretary was Father John Magee, from Newry, whose understanding of Irish Catholicism was similar to that of his fellow Northern Ireland man, Cardinal Conway.

Dr FitzGerald's meeting with His Holiness took place in the papal study decorated with teak and modern art, and filled with books, prominent among them being the works of the French Catholic philosopher, Jacques Maritain, one of which, *The Three Masters,* was translated by Paul from French into Italian.

It was to Maritain that Dr FitzGerald had looked for inspiration in developing a political philosophy applicable to Irish Catholicism. Dr FitzGerald's choice of Maritain was doubly apt. Firstly, Bishop Newman of Limerick had considered Maritain to have been in error on some matters. Secondly, Paul VI was an admirer and follower of Maritain.

Maritain had argued that the concrete historical ideal of the modern age must be marked first and foremost by pluralism, particularly in the religious sphere. It was Maritain's thesis that the domain of the temporal must be granted due autonomy. There had to be full religious freedom. Temporal authority, having become closely dependent on the consent of the governed, had to endeavour to respect all differences in the social scene. The society of the future therefore would be a variegated one, a multiplicity of very different and sometimes clashing interests that must try to live together in fraternal community.

While Paul VI liked intellectual ideas he found it hard to make decisions. It was Archbishop Benelli, as the right hand man of the Pope since 1967, whom Dr FitzGerald had to convince, if there was to be a positive response to his presentation. In a series of articles on Benelli's influence which appeared in the *Observer* in 1973, Peter Hebblethwaite had described the remarkable power which he yielded as the Substitute Secretary of State. According to Hebblethwaite, Benelli was unsympathetic to much of the thinking of Vatican II and favoured Vatican centralism rather than devolving powers to the national episcopal conferences. In his book, *The Anatomy of the Vatican*, Paul Hoffman describes Benelli as a blunt Tuscan who handled all the really important church business. "The reports, complaints, and requests from the world's Roman Catholic bishops sooner or later came to his desk, along with memos, drafts and documents that are the steady output of the Church's administrative mills".

Benelli, who had worked in the Dublin nunciature as a young man, had a high regard for Cardinal Conway and for his strategy of controlled change. He had studied Dr FitzGerald's written presentations carefully. A bad omen for pluralism in Ireland was that Benelli had directed the Holy See to fight against the introduction of divorce in Italy.

We can reconstruct the substance of Dr FitzGerald's presentation from two major speeches which he had made in Dublin: the first was the 1976 speech on pluralism; the second was an 1974 address to an international consultation on mixed marriages.

Pluralism: Dr FitzGerald explained the case for the removal from the constitution and laws of the Republic aspects which were unduly influenced by the Catholic Church. These could include:

1. Modifications in the national school system, dominated by the Churches, with a view to ensuring that where a sufficient group of parents seek mixed rather than denominational education, their needs would so far as possible be met.

2. Repeal of article 41 of the constitution forbidding legislation for the dissolution of marriage and, after careful study of the legal complexities involved, a review of existing civil laws of marriage designed at least to remove present anomalies arising from the different civil and ecclesiastical codes.

3. Reform of the law on contraception.

4. Finding the broadest possible consensus to oppose abortion.

Mixed Marriages: This was the subject most stressed by Dr FitzGerald in his verbal presentation. He argued that political problems arose in the case of mixed marriages in the Republic, with a 96 per cent Roman Catholic population and in Northern Ireland with its 35 per cent Roman Catholic population. Between 1946 and 1961 about a quarter of Protestants in the Republic had married Catholics. Many of these were Protestant males, whose wives had handed on the Roman Catholic faith to the children. Along with a higher death rate among Protestants, mixed marriages had contributed to an erosion of the Protestant population by about 25 per cent per generation - or around one per cent per annum. According to Dr FitzGerald no similar phenomenon appeared to exist, at any rate on such a scale, anywhere else in the world.

In Northern Ireland the social pressures against mixed marriage were stronger and more dangerous - some individuals had paid with their lives because they committed the offence of a mixed marriage.

"The consequence of the existence of these two very different situations in the two parts of this island, has been that Protestants in Northern Ireland have observed a continuous decline in the number of their co-religionists in the Republic.

"There have been many pogroms of Roman Catholics in Northern Ireland over the years - within the past five years tens of thousands of Roman Catholic families have had to leave their homes. The proximate cause of these tragic events lies in the IRA campaign of the past four years, but the ultimate cause is the fear amongst Protestants of absorption in a predominantly Roman Catholic Ireland in which, they believe, they would disappear as rapidly as Protestants have been disappearing in the Republic for decades past.

"There is thus the paradox that the Roman Catholic Church's policy with respect to mixed marriages when it operates in the kind of conditions that exist in the Republic, though presumably having the intended effect of maximising the Roman Catholic population in that area, also has the effect of helping to threaten the very existence of the Roman Catholic population in parts of Northern Ireland".

Dr FitzGerald also raised the more fundamental question of how the discouragement of inter-marriage - and of mixed schooling - contributed to inter-community strife in Northern Ireland:

"The failure of the settlers in the north-east and the native

57

Irish in this area to assimilate was not in earlier centuries due to particular ecclesiastical legislation with regard to mixed marriages, for this legislation became a significant factor only after *Ne Temere* was promulgated in Ireland in 1908. But it is arguable that this application of these new and stringent requirements with respect to the religious upbringing of the children of mixed marriages in the early years of the twentieth century, came at a crucial point in Irish history and probably contributed to continuing the division of two sections of the community at a time of particular political tension. Certainly positive encouragement of mixed marriages, rather than discouragement, would have been more likely to have improved community relations in Northern Ireland during this century, although another important factor in the maintenance of the lethal division between two sections of the Northern Ireland community can also be argued to have been the segregation of children for educational purposes".

The Pope listened to Dr Fitzgerald's arguments, but being an even more experienced diplomat than either Benelli or Casaroli, his response was inscrutable. We do not know what is recorded, if anything, in the Vatican archives and in the archives of the Department of Foreign Affairs in Dublin. If further developments were contemplated, circumstances changed quickly. Within weeks Cardinal Conway was dead, Archbishop Benelli was made Cardinal Archbishop of Florence by Paul VI in June, and in July, Dr FitzGerald lost office in the Fianna Fáil land-slide victory. Above all, in August 1978 Pope Paul VI died. At the conclave to chose his successor Cardinal Benelli was the pope-maker who swung the vote in favour of the Cardinal Patriarch of Venice, Albino Luciani. But John Paul I, as Luciani was now known, died after only 33 days as Pope. His brief tenure of office, during which he expressed admiration for Hans Kung and showed other signs of liberal thinking, might have augured well for a Vatican reassessment of the Irish situation.

This reassessment was not to be forthcoming under the third Pope of 1978, Karol Wojtyla, who defeated Cardinal Benelli at the conclave which gave the Catholic Church its first non-Italian Pope in 455 years. "It is as if to confront an unprecedented religious crisis, the cardinals preferred the human and spiritual qualities of a Polish combatant to the qualities of ecclesiastical diplomacy which had characterised the previous pontificates", Alain Woodrow wrote in *Le Monde*.

In *The Pope's Divisions* Mr Peter Nichols suggested that "John Paul was the answer to the conclave's belief that the Catholic Church needed taking in hand, and that its long-period of unease, confusion, experiments, of doubts and dis-cussions, to say nothing of defections, which had begun with the later years of Pius XII and culminated in the Vatican Council, had now to be brought to an end".

The Pope of the Restoration quickly established his author-ity. He committed himself - and therefore the Catholic Church - on a range of subjects which were the subject of heated debate under Paul VI: he upheld the condemnation of artificial birth control, he opposed the ordination of women to the priesthood, he attacked divorce and abortion while denouncing the evils of consumerism in the West. Part of his strong appeal stemmed from his attempts to restore confi-dence and certitude among Catholics after the uncertainty and infighting that marked the Church in the aftermath of Vatican II. He was to be a travelling Pope.

There were intensive preparations for the Pope's visit to Ireland in September 1979. Dr FitzGerald, now the leader of Fine Gael, revived his idea of asking Pope John Paul to con-sider the special conditions in Ireland in regard to mixed mar-riages. His earlier initiative may have been known from the government's private files. In any case, Dr FitzGerald disco-vered that the Taoiseach, Mr Lynch, shared this intent.

The two political leaders agreed to make a joint approach. But that case was not to be made. Apparently, the Pope arrived late for his meeting with them at the nuncio's residence in Cabra, and there was not enough time to raise the matter.

Whether Pope John Paul II would have listened to them sympathetically is doubtful. The Pope had his own conception of Ireland as a Catholic nation and of the road ahead which it must follow. In his speech in Limerick Pope John Paul said: "Ireland must choose. You the present generation of Irish people must decide; your choice must be clear and your decision firm. Let the voice of your forefathers, who suffered so much to maintain their faith in Christ and thus to preserve Ireland's soul, resound today in your ears through the voice of the Pope when he repeats the words of Christ: 'What will it profit a man, if he gains the whole world, and forfeits his life? What would it profit Ireland to go the easy way of the world and suffer the loss of her own soul?"

The uneasy way prescribed by Pope John Paul was to revere and protect the family and family life. "Divorce, for whatever reason it is introduced, inevitably becomes easier and easier to obtain and it gradually comes to be accepted as a normal part of life. The very possibility of divorce in the sphere of civil law makes stable and permanent marriages more difficult for everyone. May Ireland always continue to give witness before the modern world to her traditional commitment, corresponding to the true dignity of man, to the sanctity and the indissolubility of the marriage bond".

John Paul's message was delivered in Limerick. The thinking of Bishop Jeremiah Newman, which had been to the right of the 1973 episcopal guidelines drawn-up by Cardinal Conway, and who was the arch-opponent of Dr FitzGerald's pluralist society, was now mainstream orthodoxy as far as the Pope was concerned.

Chapter 4

ABORTION

After Mass in a County Kerry church attended by the papal
nuncio, Dr. Gaetano Alibrandi, a Dominican priest invoked
the defeat of the Turks by the Christians at the Battle of
Lepanto in 1571 to rally the faithful of Ireland in the autumn
of 1983. There would be an event as important as the battle of
Lepanto taking place in Ireland on September 7th, he
prophesied. "On that day the world will be watching Ireland,
and I want you to say your rosary all day long and, if possible,
in front of the Blessed Sacrament".

The crusade was on but it was not the constitutional one
envisaged by Garret FitzGerald in his RTÉ radio interview.
As the Tánaiste, Dick Spring, was to remark, it was the most
bitter and divisive event in Irish history : "neighbour has
turned against neighbour; eminent professional men have bit-
terly denounced each other in public; the Churches could
hardly be further apart; colleagues in the same political party
have launched personal attacks on each other".

At the head of this other crusade was the Bishop of Kerry,
Dr. Kevin McNamara, who a few days after the Dominican's
Lepanto appeal attended a meeting in a convent in the small
town of Millstreet in the neighbouring county of Cork. Dr.
McNamara spoke to members of seventeen local branches of
the pro-life movement about "the great issue of our time", of
whether Ireland would become a country in which the slaugh-
ter of unborn children would become an accepted fact or
whether the Irish people would meet the challenge of caring
for pregnant women so that they would not resort to abortions. The bishop warned that a strong pro-abortion lobby
existed in Ireland with powerful backing in the media and
with the support of the international pro-abortion interest. If
those opposed to abortion lost on September 7th this would

be interpreted as paving the way for the legalisation of abortion in Ireland within five years.

On September 7th 1983 the Irish people were asked to give their verdict on the Eighth Amendment to the Constitution, which proposed the additional insertion that "The State acknowledges the right to life of the unborn and, with due regard to the right to life of the mother, guarantees in its laws to respect, and, as far as practicable, by its laws to defend and vindicate that right".

Although abortion is illegal in Ireland under an Act of 1861, official statistics showed that some 3,500 women a year travelled to Britain to end pregnancies. Such statistics were viewed with shame and horror in a society with a profound aversion to abortion. Apart from minority groups such as the feminist Right to Choose organisation, public opinion was staunchly against any liberalisation of abortion. No politician of note advocated legalisation of abortion. Remarkably, however, the highly emotional issue of "murdering babies" became a long-drawn-out issue in Irish politics and society during a campaign which all too often presented the controversy as being "for" or "against" abortion. Such a simplistic presentation concealed more fundamental and complex attitudes toward social change. It was also a campaign which resulted in the insertion of a clause into the constitution which the Catholic bishops saw as a human rights clause but which the leaders of the other churches deemed to be sectarian.

The idea that a constitutional amendment would be required to prevent abortion being made legal by the courts was mooted by Father Maurice Dooley, a moral theologian in an article in 1974 in *Social Studies*. The possibility was raised at a conference on medical ethics in September 1980 organised by a Scotsman, Dr. John Bonnar, Professor of Obstetrics at Trinity College, Dublin. This led, in early 1981, to the formation of the Pro-Life Amendment Campaign, (PLAC) which brought together various right-wing Catholic groups eager to press for an amendment to the constitution guaranteeing the right to life of the unborn. Because of an unprecedented spate of elections — there were three in 18 months — the Campaign had a phenomenal success in eliciting promises from the politicians.

The Pro-Life Amendment Campaign was launched officially in Buswell's Hotel, just a stone's throw from Leinster House, on April 27th 1981. Its first meeting was chaired by Dr. Julia Vaughan, a former nun, and was attended by many notable gynaecologists including Professor Eamon de Valera. With an election known to be imminent, the Campaign decided to seek the backing of the politicians for their proposal.

The first politican to be canvassed for support was Dr. Garret FitzGerald who was leader of Fine Gael, which party he had modernised and reshaped in a social democratic direction since taking over in 1977 from Mr. Cosgrave. Only a few weeks earlier Marie Stack, a member of Young Fine Gael and a newly appointed vice-president of the party, had made some remarks on abortion which were seized upon by Fianna Fáil as advocating abortion. Such an incident had warned the Fine Gael leadership of how the abortion issue could flare up in a way which too easily could dub the party as permissive, in contrast to the pro-family traditionalism of Fianna Fáil. Furthermore, Dr. FitzGerald was personally opposed to abortion, as instanced in his 1975 speech in which he had urged politicians and churchmen to find common ground against any legalisation of abortion.

Accordingly, Dr. FitzGerald responded positively to PLAC's proposition that there was a danger of the Supreme Court permitting abortion against the wishes of the Dáil. As there was no disagreement among the different religious faiths against abortion, it seemed to Dr. FitzGerald that the proposal was reasonable. A firm commitment appeared in the June 1981 Fine Gael election literature: "Fine Gael is unalterably opposed to the legalisation of abortion and in goverment will initiate a referendum to guarantee the right to life of the unborn child."

The Taoiseach, Mr. Haughey, who had succeeded Mr. Lynch in December 1979, was more circumspect than Dr. FitzGerald and did not give a specific undertaking to PLAC at his first meeting with campaigners. Soon afterwards, however, Mr. Haughey gave Dr. Vaughan "a solemn assurance" that Fianna Fáil would introduce an amendment if returned to office after the election. The then Labour leader, Mr. Frank

Cluskey, did not give PLAC any specific commitment but said he was sympathetic to that objective.

In June 1981 Dr. FitzGerald became Taoiseach in a coalition government with Labour, but in the Joint Programme of Government there was no reference to the holding of a pro-life referendum. A main concern was to deal with the country's worsening economic crisis. That autumn Dr. FitzGerald launched the Constitutional Crusade. PLAC was not enamoured of the prospect of its proposal being dealt with in such a wide review of the constitution. When Dr. Vaughan approached Dr. FitzGerald, he informed her that work on the wording was being undertaken by the Attorney General, Mr. Peter Sutherland, but that this was a difficult process.

The collapse of Dr. FitzGerald's administration in January 1982 provided PLAC with the opportunity to remount its campaign. Mr. Haughey promised to enact the amendment in 1982, while Dr. FitzGerald promised there would be a referendum during the lifetime of the next Dáil. Mr. Haughey became Taoiseach again in March but his administration fell in October. Only two days before the collapse of the 23rd Dáil, the Minister for Health, Dr. Michael Woods, produced the wording that "this State acknowledges the right to life of the unborn and with due regard to the right to life of the mother guarantees in its laws to respect, and as far as is practicable, by its laws to defend and vindicate that right".

Although that wording was not opposed by Dr. FitzGerald, the Fine Gael leader was viewed with some suspicion by PLAC, especially in view of an interview the previous March in which he said that it would be a mistake to hold a pro-life referendum in isolation from other constitutional amendments. PLAC successfully lobbied delegates to the Fine Gael Ard Fheis in October and ensured the defeat of a motion calling for a deferral of the referendum.

The new Joint Fine Gael-Labour Programme for Government pledged: "Legislation will be introduced to have adopted by March 31st, 1983, the pro-life amendment published by the outgoing government, which has the backing of the two largest parties in the Dáil. The Parliamentary Labour Party reserves the right to a free vote on this issue".

The party whips agreed to introduce the bill on budget day,

February 9th, 1983. The Minister for Justice, Michael Noonan, announced that the government would consider changes in the wording of the proposed amendment, provided they retained the underlying principle that the practice of abortion should not be permitted to creep into Irish law. Mr. Noonan stressed that in approving the principle of the bill, the Dáil would not be commiting itself to the particular wording of that bill, nor to any other particular wording. Most importantly, Mr. Noonan explained that recent questions had arisen as to whether the wording could cause unforeseen difficulties. His advice had shown that, on one interpretation, the amendment could positively facilitate the introduction of abortion on a wide scale.

This was a clear signal that the government would not rush the legislation through and that it did not feel bound to hold a referendum by the promised date of March 31st. The Fianna Fáil spokesman, Michael Woods, defended his party's wording as having taken full account of Protestant thinking on the subject. "Indeed I would have to say that at the time the amendment was published we were entitled to believe that we had secured the general support and agreement of the Church of Ireland and of the Catholic Church at the highest levels and either a benevolent attitude or at least a lack of opposition from most of the other Churches," he said.

In Galway the following week-end at a Young Fine Gael Conference - which overwhelmingly opposed the adoption of any constitutional amendment - Dr. FitzGerald explained his misgivings. Further consideration would have to be given to legal difficulties that had been identified in the proposed amendment. But this overture from the Taoiseach was rebuffed by Fianna Fáil which insisted that its wording should remain unchanged.

The alternative wording produced by Fine Gael proposed "Nothing in this Constitution shall be invoked to invalidate or to deprive of force or effect, any provision of a law on the grounds that it prohibits abortion".

On April 28th in the Dáil the Fine Gael amendment was defeated by 87 to 63 votes. The final stage with the original - the Fianna Fáil - wording was then passed by 85 to 11. Despite Dr. FitzGerald's warning of the dangers to the lives of women and advice to his party to vote against it, most of them abstained. Only Monica Barnes and Alan Shatter voted against. In the Senate there was eloquent opposition to the amendment from Mary Robinson, Michael D. Higgins, Catherine McGuinness, Brendan Ryan, John Robb, Shane Ross and Katherine Bulbulia.

The Attorney General, Mr. Sutherland, had advised the government that the Fianna Fáil wording left uncertain the question of life to be protected - that of the mother or the child - thus making it possible that abortion could be legalised by a decision of the courts. Sutherland, now Ireland's member of the EEC Commission in Brussels, also drew the government's attention to the probability that the wording would be interpreted by the courts to exclude operations to save the life of the mother that were being carried out in hospitals in accordance with the medical ethics and theology of all the churches. These included saving the lives of mothers in cases of ectopic pregnancies or cancer of the womb.

The Fianna Fáil wording was judged to be sectarian and divisive by the Protestant Churches. The Church of Ireland Primate, Dr. John Armstrong, suggested in an RTÉ radio interview that the campaign had echoes of the Mother and Child Scheme in so far as the moral theology of one Church was being forced on all the people, and he regretted that the amendment was cutting right across what Dr. FitzGerald's constitutional crusade was trying to do. An offical statement from Dr. Armstrong and the Archbishop of Dublin, Dr. Henry McAdoo, reiterated the Church of Ireland view that abortion may be required in certain medical circumstances but that voting on the referendum wording was a matter for the individual's conscience.

The General Assembly of the Presbyterian Church of June 1982 adopted a resolution expressing firm opposition to "indiscriminate abortion", but added that "it does not believe it is wise to insert a clause banning abortion into the constitution of the Irish Republic. The State's regulation of this and other matters affecting morals should be a matter for legislation by the Dáil and the Senate and not for definition in the constitution". This resolution was reaffirmed a year later at the 1983 assembly in Dublin.

66

The Methodist Church's Council on Social Welfare stated that its main body - the Conference - had been firmly opposed to indiscriminate abortion but believed that the State's regulation of this and other matters affecting morals in the Republic should be a matter for legislation by the Oireachtas and not for definition in the constitution. The statement also pointed out that a decision to support the amendment must be made in the full recognition that such a vote was a rejection of the Protestant Churches' position. Earlier the Council had circulated a warning to TDs and Senators that the insertion of an inflexible "Roman Catholic clause" would be sectarian.

The Rev Ian Paisley, who combines leadership of the Free Presbyterian Church with his commitments as a politician in the Westminster and European Parliaments, said in an *Irish Times* interview that the adoption of the amendment would be seen by him as a return to "the special position" of the Roman Catholic Church in the Republic and as strengthening "the Roman Catholic theology that underlies the 1937 constitution". Mr. Paisley endorsed the views of Protestant leaders in the Republic that abortion was not a matter to be dealt with by constitution but was an area for legislation or prohibition by democratically elected representatives in the Dáil. He dismissed Dr. FitzGerald's crusade as "the greatest non-starter the Taoiseach has ever entered into".

It was believed that the Fianna Fáil wording had been drafted at a meeting attended by Monsignor Gerard Sheehy, head of the Dublin Regional Marriage Advisory Council. On March 2nd 1983 the Catholic bishops issued a statement opposing the revised Fine Gael proposal on the grounds that it did not exclude the possibility that in the future a law could be passed by the Dáil permitting abortion in some form without a direct vote of the people. In the public perception, the Catholic bishops had sided with Fianna Fáil against Dr. FitzGerald.

Behind the scenes Dr. FitzGerald had explained his reservations about the Fianna Fáil wording to a member of the hierarchy, and had raised the possibility of holding consultations with the bishops to work out an acceptable form of wording. The word came back to Dr. FitzGerald that this should be done through an intermediary. That intermediary rejected the Fine Gael text. Later it was to be learned by Dr. FitzGerald that misunderstanding had arisen and that the intermediate discussions had gone wrong. The government understood that no other wording was acceptable to the hierarchy, whereas the hierarchy's intent was to convey to ministers that there were difficulties about this alternative wording but that further discussions could resolve these. This failure in communications was to convince Dr. FitzGerald in 1986 that talks on marriage and divorce should be directly with the bishops.

There is no evidence that the campaign was begun - or encouraged - by the bishops, though Dr. McNamara addressed a meeting of the pro-amendment side. The hierarchy's spokesman, Bishop Joseph Cassidy, said that he would go into any witness box to swear that the bishops were not behind the campaign.

However, the Church's involvement was summed up as "a Carmelite on one hand and a ballot box in the other". Throughout the land the pulpits of the Catholic Churches thundered with the simplistic message to the faithful that to vote against the amendment would be to vote for abortion. A book aimed at exploring the more complex and delicate legal and moral issues, *Abortion and Law,* was published by Dominican Publications as a *Doctrine and Life Special.* Concerned Catholics urged Cardinal Ó Fiaich and Archbishop Ryan to issue a statement recognising that Catholics in conscience were free to vote against the amendment. A number of bishops were ready to welcome such an initiative and, after a meeting of the hierachy at Maynooth - with the nuncio, Dr. Alibrandi, sitting in to hear the discussions - a statement was agreed.

Published on August 22nd 1983, the statement from the episcopal conference recognised the right of each person to vote according to conscience but said that it was its considered opinion that the amendment would safeguard the right to life both of the mother and the unborn child. "While some conscientiously hold a different opinion, we are convinced that a clear majority in favour of the amendment will greatly contribute to the continued protection of unborn human life in the laws of our country. This could have a significant impact in a world where abortion is often taken for granted. A decisive 'Yes' to the amendment will, we believe, in the words of Pope John Paul II in Limerick, constitute a 'witness before Europe and before the whole world to the dignity and sacredness of all human life, from conception until death".

Archbishop Ryan and Bishop McNamara departed from the agreed hierarchy statement and took an unqualified stance against the amendment. Dr. Ryan, in a pastoral letter read at all Masses in the Dublin diocese, said that the real issue "is ultimately one of life and death: that is, whether at some stage in the future some unborn children may be put to death in our country, rather than be allowed to live on".

This matter was so serious that it was certainly reasonable to entrust a final decision on it only to the people as a whole, the pastoral said. This was not to express distrust either in the Oireachtas or in the courts. It was rather to seek "that, in an issue as vital as this, all our people would be given their fullest possible participation in the democratic process".

Dr. McNamara, in a sermon at a special Mass in St. Mary's Cathedral, Killarney, to mark the conclusion of the Irish Medical Association's annual congress, said that to affirm the right to life of the unborn and to try to ensure that they always enjoyed the full protection of the law, was in no way to seek to impose on others the theology of one particular church. He asserted that authoritative Protestant churchmen, from their statements, clearly wished to leave the door open to selective abortion. To legalise abortion in the so-called "hard cases" was but a first step that led inevitably to abortion more or less on demand.

In a low turnout of 53.67 per cent of the electorate the proposed constitutional change was adopted by a two to one majority. There was a much narrower margin in Dublin than elsewhere. Of the 1.25 million who voted, 841,233 were in favour and 416,136 were against adoption of the amendment. Of those voting, the pro-amendment campaign won 66.45 per cent support. But only one third of the total electorate approved the constitutional change.

In *The Irish Times* Dick Walsh wrote: "The result reflects new and deep divisions between urban and rural sections of the electorate, with urban, largely middle class areas providing strongest resistance to the amendment, and predominantly rural constituencies voting 'Yes' by majorities up to 4.5 to one. In Dublin where the result was 51.6 per cent 'Yes' and 48.3 per cent 'No', five constituencies - South East, South-West, North-East, South and Dún Laoghaire - showed majorities against change. There was overwhelming support for the amendment in such areas as Donegal, Cavan-Monaghan, Mayo, Kerry, the rural parts of Cork, East Galway, and all of the Midlands".

In a broadcast Dr. FitzGerald had explained his reasons for opposing the amendment but he did not campaign against its acceptance. The Labour leader, Dick Spring, urged rejection of the amendment despite the fact that Dr. McNamara was his local bishop. Mr. Spring matched his courage with the perceptive suggestion that the campaign represented a back-lash against the slow liberalising of Irish society. It is in this context that historians will probe the significance of the Eighth Amendment campaign. It was a reaction against the liberal values which had taken root in Irish society through the media, the Second Vatican Council, the women's movement, the decisions of the High Court and Supreme Court, particularly those of Mr. Justice Kenny. It was the reaction of people of the older generation who had grown up in the closed society of pre-1960s Ireland when the authority of bishops and priests was publicly uncontested, when the Catholic Church proclaimed certitude, when the schools induced uniformity and docility, when censorship laws forbade the reading of not only foreign writers such as Balzac, Moravia, Simenon, Orwell, Greene, Gide, Graves, Proust and Hemingway, but also Irish writers such as O'Connor, O'Faoláin, O'Brien and Behan.

This reaction in Irish society was in parallel with the return to authoritarian and traditional attitudes in the pontificate of John Paul II and in the attitudes of the new "moral majority" in the United States. It was notable that American personnel, advertising techniques and dollars were used to give the campaign a brash ring of modernity.

When the stock-taking began, the results did not look so favourable to the Catholic hierarchy. Although its recommendation was accepted - Bishop Conway of Elphin had urged that a yes vote was a vote for God - the low-turn out, particularly in Dublin, showed that the bishops' influence was on the wane. As Gerry Barry wrote in the *Sunday Tribune*, "if a party's political leader had sought to mobilise his support with the unusual and emphatic words used by Archbishop Ryan he would undoubtedly be inundated with media questions about his intentions in relation to resignation".

In due course, Dr. Ryan was promoted by Pope John Paul II to head the Vatican's department for missions, and Dr. McNamara replaced him in Dublin. Although the Pope shared the simplistic view of what was at stake in the referendum, within the Secretariat of State there were officials who recognised the wider issues. These included the fact that, by suggesting that the Supreme Court and Oireachtas could not be trusted, the campaign placed a question mark over the democratic institutions of the State - a "subversive" process which politicians had hastily, perhaps thoughtlessly, acquiesced in. Other problems were the nascent anti-clericalism of those sections of the Catholic laity who were appalled by the appropriation of pulpits by those in favour of the amendment, and the deliberate ignoring of the protests of the minority Protestant Churches that the amendment was sectarian.

In 1983 the Irish Catholic Church showed that after centuries of persecution during which, in John Horgan's phrase, it had been "a majority church with a minority psychology", it had become a majority church with a majority pyschology. Was it "the last hurrah" of a certain type of Catholicism?

Chapter 5

THE NEW IRELAND FORUM

While his constitutional crusade was being thrown into disarray by the abortion referendum, Garret FitzGerald was devoting much of his time and energy as Taoiseach in pursuit of another central concern - securing peace and stability in Northern Ireland. The prospect there looked gloomy at the start of 1983. Since the fall of the Sunningdale Agreement in 1974 successive British Secretaries of State for Northern Ireland had made no progress in reconciling the unionist and nationalist communities. Mr. Haughey's breakthrough with Mrs. Thatcher had ended in mutual recrimination. In 1981 hunger strikes had polarised the two communities even further in the north. Among the increasingly alienated nationalist community the popularity of Provisional Sinn Féin was growing. The Social Democratic and Labour Party seemed to be on the decline.

In the autumn of 1982 the SDLP leader, Mr. John Hume, proposed the setting up of a Council for a New Ireland, an idea which he put to Dr. FitzGerald. In the course of preparing a series of Dimbleby lectures on Irish identities, Dr. FitzGerald's thinking had developed beyond his earlier views on confederation. He became convinced that Mr. Haughey's emphasis on the importance of the Dublin-London axis was appropriate. The basis of a new approach needed to be formulated.

In February 1983 Dr. FitzGerald invited interested political parties to Leinster House for talks on the setting up of a New Ireland Forum. Mr. Haughey welcomed the announcement but stressed that Northern Ireland was a failed political entity and that political progress could only be made in negotiations between Dublin and London. The unionists dismissed the offer as an SDLP rescue package. The onus was therefore on the four participating parties, Fine Gael, Fianna Fáil, Labour and SDLP, to come up with the first agreed statement of the constitutional nationalist position since 1920.

The Forum began its work in Dublin Castle under the chairmanship of Dr. Colm Ó hEocha, President of University College, Galway, on May 30th 1983. From the outset there were differences of emphasis in the speeches of the party leaders.

Dr. FitzGerald warned that the price of failure would be to make a bad situation worse. Success would present Britain with an opportunity to bring peace and stability to Ireland and enduring friendship to relations between the two countries. The Forum could not hold back from examining any structures or solutions that might meet the essential requirement of giving expression to, and guaranteeing, the two Irish traditions.

Mr. Haughey defined the specific aim of the Forum as constructing a basic position which could be put to an all-Ireland constitutional conference, convened by the Irish and British governments as a prelude to British withdrawal from Northern Ireland. But he also acknowledged that a degree of autonomy might be considered for the north, possibly on the basis of Scotland's position with England.

Mr. Spring began by quoting James Connolly's remark that "Ireland without her people is nothing to me". The Labour Party, he said, sought the voluntary union of all Irish people and territory. To achieve any significant progress the Forum must look to the nature of the society that could evolve on an all-Ireland basis, consider what could be done to help create the environment in which that society could develop, and consider what changes must be made in the Republic to increase the level of tolerance and understanding necessary to achieve political progress in an all-Ireland context.

Mr. Hume said that "the heart of this crisis in Ireland is the conviction - the profound and seemingly irreducible conviction - of the majority of Protestants in the north that their ethos simply would not survive in an Irish political settlement.

"The Protestant ethos I am talking about", he said, "is not merely theological, although it contains principles such as freedom of conscience which are central to that theological heritage. It contains also, and perhaps more importantly, a strong expression of political allegiance to Britain which we

73

cannot ignore and which we cannot wish away any more than unionists could wish away our deep commitment to Irish unity.

"This intractable difficulty we must face squarely in this Forum. It will not be easy for us to do so. How do we accommodate in a new definition of Irishness these uncomfortable realities? How would we propose to give to unionists an adequate sense of security - physical, religious, political, economic and cultural - in a new Ireland?

"Are we, the nationalists of Ireland, prepared to pay the painful political and economic price that this will involve? Do we have any idea of what the price will be? I fear that many of us either do not, or would prefer not to. The work of this Forum will forever deprive us of the excuse of either ignorance or distraction" Mr. Hume declared.

The Forum's early work was overshadowed by the abortion referendum. In January 1984 it hit the national headlines as a result, ironically, of a breakdown in communications with the Catholic bishops. Cardinal Ó Fiaich confirmed that an episcopal delegation would not attend a public session of the Forum. Instead the bishops issued a written submission on ecumenism, the family, pluralism, alienation of Catholics in Northern Ireland and the Catholic school system in Northern Ireland.

Coverage centred on the paper on pluralism, written anonymously but reputed to be that of the late Archbishop Ryan. It said: "A Catholic country or its government, where there is a very substantial Catholic ethos and consensus, should not feel it necessary to apologise that its legal system, constitutional or statutory, reflects Catholic values. Such a legal system may sometimes be represented as offensive to minorities, but the rights of a minority are not more sacred than the rights of the majority." Pluralism, it added, was a value subordinate to that of the common good.

This statement, *The Irish Times* commented, had an echo of Lord Craigavon's "a Protestant parliament for a Protestant people," and its political assumptions were "firmly partitionist". *The Sunday Tribune* lamented that "the entire tone of the submission dealing with pluralism reeks of intolerance and encapsulates precisely that which northern Protestants fear would prevail in a Catholic-dominated united Ireland."

The accompanying paper on the family stressed the importance of article 41 of the constitution. It made it clear that the bishops were convinced that the introduction of civil divorce would be a direct attack on the very institution of marriage, therefore on the institution of the family, and accordingly on the basic moral fibre of society.

"In making these observations", the submission concluded, the bishops were not "in any sense seeking to require that the teaching of the Catholic Church be made the criterion of constitutional law in this country. They have already publicly stated that this is neither their role nor their wish. Rather in response to the invitation of the New Ireland Forum, are they seeking to alert the civil authorities to the grave social dangers which are inherent in so many current situations which do not appear to take adequate account of the irreplaceable role of the family, based upon marriage, as the fundamental unit of our society".

Irish Press Religious Affairs Correspondent, T.P. O'Mahony, described the absence of a key distinction between Catholic moral teaching and a supportive framework of law for that teaching as the most disappointing feature of the submission. "Neither the tone nor content of the submission shows any willingness to separate the two in a way which would leave it open to the Forum to consider new legislative provisions without setting itself at loggerheads with the bishops". He wrote, "The clear implication of the submission from the bishops - both in its reference to divorce and its section on pluralism - is that Catholic moral teaching, even in the context of a new 32 county Ireland must continue to have legislative support".

The restrictive thinking of the episcopal submission showed a distinct narrowing of viewpoint compared with two notable precedents. These involved bishops representative of the old school and of the liberals. The first, Bishop Lucey of Cork said in a 1976 RTÉ television programme that in a united Ireland legislation would not have to be in accordance with Catholic principles "in the way that it has to be" in the Republic because of its predominant Catholic majority. If unity were achieved, Bishop Lucey said he would "definitely" accept legislation on such matters as contraception and divorce. A 32 county State would be pluralistic and would have to allow for the civil liberties of the various groups living within it.

The second, Bishop Peter Birch of Ossory, commenting in 1977 on the fortieth anniversary of the 1937 constitution, urged that it should be re-written and simplified. Bishop Birch also advised that Catholics "ought to be very careful that they do not depend on the law or the constitution for standards of morality". He felt that if some of the legal supports and safeguards for Catholic moral teaching disappeared that would be "a blessing in disguise" because it would be for the Church to look at the quality of its teaching and at the need to convince people that certain things were morally wrong. Nor was he as fearful as his brother bishops about the consequences of amending article 41 of the constitution which forbids the enactment of divorce legislation.

The politicians were disappointed - not only that the bishops would not attend a plenary session of the Forum but that their thinking on the Church-State relationship was so rigid. That weekend relations between politicians and the Catholic Church grew even more tense when Cardinal Ó Fiaich said in an RTÉ radio interview that membership of Sinn Féin or electoral support for it were not necessarily wrong in every circumstance. In a prompt reaction the Irish government affirmed that "ancillary political activities could never provide grounds for support of any kind for Sinn Féin".

Relations improved after the Cardinal explained that the reason why the bishops would not attend the Forum was due to an inadequate communication from the secretariat about the date. A fresh date was suggested to the Cardinal and agreement was reached for a hearing on February 9th 1984 in Dublin Castle. Skilfully, politely and often entertainingly the four bishops - Cahal and Edward Daly, Joseph Cassidy and Dermot O'Mahony - dealt with questions from the SDLP deputy leader, Séamus Mallon, Labour's Mary Robinson, the Fianna Fáil deputy leader, Brian Lenihan, and Mr. John Kelly of Fine Gael. As Mr. Kelly remarked, this was the first time since St. Patrick arrived in Ireland that members of the hierarchy were asked to think on their feet. The public watched the performance live on television as if it were a Dallas showdown between J.R. Ewing and Cliff Barnes. According to Bishop Cassidy, the public could observe that bishops were "rather a benign species".

The drama of the occasion was heightened at the outset when Bishop Cahal Daly, whose diocese of Down and Connor includes Belfast, read out a declaration on Church-State relations. The bishops did not seek "a Catholic state for a Catholic people"; it was the business of the legislators to formulate proposals for constitutional change or to draft blueprints for a united Ireland. The bishops would resist any constitutional proposals which might infringe or endanger the civil and religious liberties cherished by northern Protestants.

These assurances were welcomed by the politicians, who detected little softening in the bishops' attitude towards divorce when Bishop Daly emphasised the hierarchy's opposition to it on pastoral grounds.

The critical exchange came when Mr. Kelly argued that there were two stages to the divorce question: firstly, the removal in a referendum of the constitutional prohibition, and secondly, perhaps several years later, the enactment of legislation to deal with marriage breakdown. As the first stage was a neutral process would the bishops give an assurance that they would not use their weight against the move?

Bishop Daly said that it was up to the politicians to frame the proposal and that if there were consequences for the moral life of society the bishops would state their views while respecting the consciences of the legislators.

An auxiliary bishop of Dublin, Dr. Dermot O'Mahony, advocated finding alternatives in marital breakdown to divorce through, for instance, closing the gap between ecclesiastical and civil nullity. But he did not want this to be so extensive as to be divorce by another name. Mr. Kelly did not see this as helping most people whose marriages were broken or on the rocks.

Earlier, however, Dr. O'Mahony assured Mr. Séamus Mallon, the deputy leader of the SDLP, that he could say absolutely that there was no danger to the civil and religious rights of Protestants in Northern Ireland. Mr. Mallon had asked if the delegation could envisage a situation where northerners would be asked to live in a new Ireland which diminished their access to divorce in law.

Dr. O'Mahony told Senator Mary Robinson that the introduction of divorce had a multiplier effect. The no-fault divorce procedure could create so much injustice. Bishop Cassidy said that Jesus Christ was against divorce and that while the common good might be faceless it was in the interest of society to defend marriage.

Northern Ireland was cited by Dr. Cahal Daly as an instance of where the widening of divorce legislation had resulted in a three-fold increase in the number of divorces in the past five years.

The briefest interviewer, taking only five minutes, was Mr. Lenihan. He asked if he would be correct to summarise the views of the bishops that they had a part to play in the pastoral and spiritual spheres, but that it was the politicians' and the legislators' task to devise the appropriate political, constitutional and legal structures for a new Ireland, taking into account what the bishops had said.

"And also the views of the other Churches and of people who dissent from our position on this matter", replied Dr. Cahal Daly.

The bishops succeeded in removing the bad impression which had been created by their written submission, but they did not succeed in removing doubts about their attitude to pluralism. Few of the politicians who left Dublin Castle that day had any doubts that the bishops would oppose a move to introduce divorce in the Republic. Behind "the father trendy" friendliness was the veiled crozier. One influential politician later commented that "the bishops were well prepared and were very skilful. They did not, however, reconcile under pressure their support of civil rights for Protestants in a united Ireland but not in the Republic".

The performance of the Catholic bishops at the Forum did not heal the hurt felt by the Protestant Churches from the anti-abortion referendum. Senator Robinson suggested that the country might have been saved from a very divisive and painful experience if the issue had been discussed at a genuine inter-church meeting, where an agreed formula might have been reached. Father Mícheál Ledwith, an expert on

78

ecumenism, admitted that it might have been handled in such a way but stressed that the differences between the churches were not easily resolved on such a fundamental matter.

Nor did the bishops make any concessions on the vexed question of mixed marriages. Dr. Cassidy revealed that the hierarchy had considered - but rejected - the possibility of asking the Vatican to relax the application of the rules in Ireland. The particular source of hurt to Protestants is the rule requiring the Catholic partner to give a verbal promise to do all in his or her power to bring up the children as Catholics.

Despite the promise being an irritant to Protestants, the bishops had decided that it would be dishonest to pass the odium to Rome. "If we felt that there was the slightest chance that there would be a change in what applies in the universal Church we would have appealed for it", Dr. Cassidy said.

The hierarchy's delegation had been asked by Mr. John Kelly of Fine Gael whether, in view of the profound disappointment of the Protestant Churches with a new directory on mixed marriages, the Catholic bishops should seek a special rule tailored to Irish conditions. A similar suggestion had also been made by Senator Mary Robinson.

Bishop Cassidy was not pressed on the details of the directory, which had come into force in November 1983 and which expressed the promise in a stronger form than is to be found in the bishops' 1976 directory. The 1983 formulation stipulates that the promise is made "as God's law requires". This is a perception of divine law not shared by the Protestant Churches.

As to the contributions to the Forum from the Church of Ireland, and the Presbyterian and Methodist Churches, Paul Arthur, of the University of Ulster, noted that they "testified eloquently of their fears and of their sense of diminished identity in the Republic". Canon Eric Elliott, a member of the Church of Ireland delegation, observed that there were present "in southern society attitudes and structures and values and definitions of identity and attitudes to religion and culture and language and history which would make it impossible for me to identify totally with that situation in terms of my own identity, my own security and my own assurance".

Similarly, the Presbyterian Synod of Dublin pointed out

that a "number of issues in the constitution, in law, and in practice have developed in such a way as to reflect the overwhelming outlook of the population. The areas which need re-examination and action include marriage, law, adoption, family planning, medical ethics and education".

But a broader perspective was submitted to the Forum by the Irish Theological Association, a predominantly Catholic body. Its submission, which has been published in the book, *Irish Challenges to Theology,* declared that "the civil law is the business of the State, not the Churches", and that it was never justified for the laws of a State to be those of a particular Church, even a minority Church.

The Theological Association observed that it was commonly believed "with some justification" that since partition, the Catholic Church had enjoyed too close relations with the State in the Republic, while the Protestant Churches had been too close to the State in the North. In a new Ireland such a close connection between Church and State would not be acceptable to their mutual advantage.

"We are a society with different cultural, political and religious traditions", the association declared. "This is a fact of pluralism. What we are to do about this fact is the moral challenge of pluralism. North and south the temptation has been to ignore the fact and so equivalently to suppress the weaker traditions. This is no longer acceptable on moral and Christian, any more than on political grounds. We must go beyond mere tolerance by cherishing the diversity".

80

Chapter 6

THE CHANGING AND UNCHANGING CHURCH

Although it was not admitted publicly, the absence of the Catholic bishops from all official ceremonies hosted by the FitzGerald government during the visit in June 1984 of President Ronald Reagan and his wife, Nancy, was no coincidence. It was an episcopal boycott of the political leader of the western world. While President Reagan traced his Ballyporeen roots in Tipperary, attended a State reception in Dublin Castle, and addressed the Dáil, the "benign species" went missing either to the Scottish island of Iona or to confirmation engagements. The hierarchy showed solidarity for Bishop Eamonn Casey rather than deference to President Reagan. The absence of the bishops signified their support as individuals for Bishop Casey's call for Ireland to show its solidarity with the oppressed in countries such as Nicaragua and El Salvador.

Exception to a suggestion that the hierarchy had moved to the left on such an issue was taken by Bishop Newman, who insisted that the bishops were not anti-American. Bishop Newman, however, was missing the point that not so long ago American Presidents would have been greeted by Irish bishops as leaders of the free world against atheistic communism. Instead, in 1984, the Irish bishops were indicating their criticism of American infringement of human rights of the people of Central America.

Viewed in the context of earlier decades, this change in outlook of the hierarchy was revolutionary but it had been evolving steadily over the previous two decades, though it had developed momentum in recent years. At the source of this transformation were the teachings of the Second Vatican Council, which emphasised that involvement for social justice was an integral duty of the Christian alongside spiritual development.

81

An early manifestation of this reassessment came with the protests against the Vietnam War led by Daniel and Philip Berrigan. Although they encountered opposition, not only from the US political establishment but also from church authorities, the Berrigans inspired countless Catholics in the United States and elsewhere, including Ireland.

Practical effect to the teaching of Vatican Two was given in Ireland in 1973 when Cardinal Conway established Trócaire to express the Irish Catholic Church's concern for promoting justice and peace in the Third World, and, as importantly, of educating the Irish people on the realities of life in the Third World. Of immense importance in achieving this objective have been Bishop Casey, Trócaire's chairman, and its director, Mr. Brian McKeown.

Simultaneously, Irish priests and nuns in missionary countries have been influenced by their experience and have espoused liberation theology. Their new awareness of the social gospel is being transported back to Ireland, which before Vatican Two had been reputed for clerical authoritarianism. This new Irish missionary outlook was personified by Father Niall O'Brien of the Negros Nine in the Philippines.

The missionary influence is now being felt throughout the Irish Church. Within the hierarchy, Bishop James Kavanagh had spoken out on behalf of Nicky Kelly, Bishop Dermot O'Mahony was involved in seeking a solution to the H-block hunger-strikes in 1981 and Bishop Donal Murray helped draft a bishops' letter on the arms race. Symptomatic of the changing outlook of the younger bishops was the remark by Bishop Brendan Comiskey of Ferns that today's bishop should have the Bible in one hand and an ESRI report in the other. Within the clergy, the Association of Irish Priests has begun to take a more critical look at Irish society, identifying unemployment as the main challenge to Christians. Individual priests and nuns have engaged in "neighbourhood" Christian living, Jesuits such as Peter McVerry have opposed the Criminal Justice Act, while priests and nuns have taken up the cause of the travelling people.

At the theological level, the Irish Theological Association is trying to develop distinctive Irish theology that would learn from the Latin American and German liberation theologians but which would be based on Irish conditions, not least in response to the sectarian violence in Northern Ireland and the growing secularisation of life both north and south.

Thus, in the words of the German theologian, Johann Baptist Metz, Irish theologians are striving to create a "church of the people" rather than a "church for the people". The champions of such an outlook would refashion the essentially nineteenth century structure of Irish Catholicism into a "basic community" Church, as advocated by Peadar Kirby in his book, *"Is Irish Catholicism dying?"* This "basic community" Church co-exists with the more paternalist and traditionalist church which faces unprecedented challenges from the secularisation of society.

The 1960s were a watershed in Irish history. Economic and social change was rapidly transforming the Republic. Prosperity had arrived, as witness Brian Cleeve's novel *Cry of Morning,* a novel about the new Irish revolution - of money and expensive cars and towering office blocks among the Georgian slums of an expanding Dublin. Young Irish people needed no longer to go to London for city life. They could head for Dublin and experience the freedom of anonymous city life away from the social constraints of village life.

The focus and the stimulator of much of this new revolution was television. In 1961 RTÉ received its charter. Undoubtedly the influence of RTÉ - and of the BBC in the parts of Ireland where it can be "picked-up" - has been colossal in opening up for discussion subjects previously considered taboo. Programmes like Gay Byrne's *The Late Late Show* and *Here and Now* presented by Liam Nolan and Rodney Rice had immeasurable influence in broadening the outlook of Irish people.

Simultaneously, a revolution took place in Irish newspapers. The old magisterial anonymity and cultivated detachment gave way to a more lively and personal presentation. Under the editorship of Douglas Gageby and the news editorship of Donal Foley, *The Irish Times* became an important formative influence on the outlook of a section of the Irish public, particularly on professional, business and student readers. Significantly, too, *The Irish Times* which had been considered the organ of the Anglo-Irish ascendancy widened out its policy - and its appeal.

In 1971 Mr. Louis McRedmond, an experienced commentator on religion, wrote that it was his impression that between 20 per cent and 30 per cent of young people in the 20 to 35 age group was either lapsed from the Catholic faith or in danger of lapsing. In 1974 a major survey by the hierarchy's Research and Development Unit showed that 91 per cent of Catholics were attending Sunday Mass. This high figure was described by Bishop Cahal Daly as reassuring. That survey also showed that 65 per cent went to Communion monthly, 95 per cent believed in the existence of God, 95 per cent believed in Christ and his Church and 90 per cent believed in the presence of Christ in the Eucharist. A closer examination of the findings led Professor Liam Ryan of Maynooth to conclude that the statistics were less reassuring for the Church authorities. Over one-third of the respondents reported that religious principles seldom if ever guided their behaviour, a figure which rose to 55 per cent for city-born and to 61 per cent for the under 30 age group.

Professor Ryan detected the emergence of a new type of Irish Catholic, as yet in a minority, characterised by an informed appreciation of the value of the supernatural and sacramental life of the Catholic Church but retaining an independence of mind largely on moral matters. Furthermore, only a minority of Irish Catholics fully accepted their Church's prohibition on divorce and contraception, Professor Ryan wrote in the January 1983 issue of *The Furrow*. But there was a strong rejection of abortion. This new type of Catholic demanded that the Church speak out on matters of social morality but not on moral matters affecting his or her personal life.

The observation of Professor Ryan assumes great significance when account is taken of the fact that the Republic, with a population of 3.5 million, has the youngest population in the EEC with 48 per cent under the age of 25 years, as well as the lowest proportion over 65. In 1982 the Republic had the highest birth rate in the EEC with 20.4 live births per 1,000 of the population. But the family size, which averaged 3.5 in 1971, is falling. During the present recession a major problem of an Irish government is to provide jobs for this expanding young population. The resumption of emigration is a sad barometer of government failure to create these jobs.

An update of the 1974 survey was published by the bishops in 1985. It showed a small decrease - from 91 per cent to 87 per cent - in Mass attendance. Over the decade there has been a movement away from full acceptance of various church teachings to qualified acceptance or uncertainty. Nearly 30 per cent, for instance, now have difficulty in believing papal infallibility compared with 18 per cent in 1974. The findings also showed that difficulties with church teachings were mainly in the sphere of sexual morality. On divorce, 43 per cent "agreed", and 48 per cent "disagreed" with the statement that "divorce should never be allowed". Eleven years ago 54% had agreed and 41% had disagreed. In 1985 the proportion of "don't knows" (9%) was almost double that in 1974.

The clear shift towards more permissive attitudes to sex, drugs, divorce and homosexuality among young people is also confirmed from data collected early in 1981 and published in the 1984 *European Value Systems Survey*. Various surveys have raised questions about the extent to which religious education is imparting a coherent belief system to young persons.

While Ireland remains a conspicuous church-going country, attendance is on the decline. "The decline is very noticeable in centre-city churches on weekdays", observes Father Austin Flannery OP. "Twenty years ago they would have been thronged with early morning worshippers, young and old. Nowadays the early morning Masses are attended by but handfuls of people, mostly middle-aged and old. On Sunday Mass attendance is very high but fewer young people go to church".

In a booklet on *The future of the faith,* a text which he wrote for the Vatican Secretariat for Non-believers, Bishop Donal Murray concluded that "if there are, as all the signs show, increasing numbers of young people, of unemployed, of women, and indeed of the whole community, who see the Church as having little to say to their lives and concerns and as offering little challenge to them, then it is clear that the notion of what the Church is about needs to be expanded and enriched for them as a matter of the utmost urgency".

Dr. Gabriel Daly OSA told the annual meeting of the Theological Association that just as it was not Wolfe Tone's republicanism which had triumphed after the War of Independence, the Roman Catholicism which had the hold on the nation's conscience was not that of Vatican Two but was inward-looking, triumphalist, philistine and unecumenical ."We continue to pay the price for our former authoritarianism and uncritical faith", he said. "The signs are that an increasing number of our people are passing from a totally uncritical faith to a totally uncritical unbelief".

Twenty one years after the ending of the Second Vatican Council, the Irish bishops have not evolved structures to involve the laity in the running of the Church. Meetings of the hierarchy take place in private at Maynooth, and there has been nothing similar to the Liverpool Congress of bishops, priests and laity. The Vatican Council principle of coresponsibility has been ignored. Bishops remain an exclusive elite appointed in secrecy by Rome, giving some substance to Dr. Noel Browne's charge at the 1985 MacGill Summer School that they are colonial governors for Rome Rule.

No appointment by a Pope is as decisive for the official direction of the Irish Church as is the appointment of the Archbishop of Dublin, the largest diocese in the Republic and the diocese which is closest to the centre of Government. Dr. Kevin McNamara is John Paul ll's man. Born in County Clare in 1926, Dr. McNamara was a professor of theology at Maynooth College during the changes brought about by the Second Vatican Council. Having grown up under two authoritarian Popes, Pius Xl and Pius Xll, he adjusted to the new pastoral style papacy of John XXlll. Colleagues recall that in the period after Vatican ll he was affected by the conciliarism of the time. Before Paul Vl's condemnation of artificial forms of birth control, Dr. McNamara was considered to be among those theologians who expected a change and he was suspect as a liberal by the Maynooth old-guard. With the publication of *Humanae Vitae,* Dr. McNamara's theology took the more definite shape of certitude for which he is now publicly renowned: had Paul Vl changed the teaching on birth control, it would have been clear that the Catholic Church was in truth no longer the same Church, he was to write later.

In Poland Karol Wojtyla and in Germany Joseph Ratzinger were drawing similar conclusions about the need to put the brakes on experimentation.

In 1975 Kevin McNamara became Bishop of Kerry. He excelled as a pastoral bishop, quickly winning the affection and loyalty of the clergy and people. He also became known nationally as the outspoken critic of "the contraceptive mentality". Along with Dr. Ryan he was a staunch supporter of the 1983 amendment against abortion.

In Kerry, as in Maynooth, the two sides of Kevin McNamara coexisted: there was the quiet, unassuming Clareman who could sit happily in a parish hall with a cup of tea in hand, listening attentively to what everyone had to say; then there was the torrential outpouring in print from the hierarchy's preeminent public polemicist.

"McNamara's band is coming to Dublin" was the word that spread around Leinster House the evening before his appointment as Archbishop of Dublin was announced in November 1984. The news broke just as the Taoiseach, Dr. FitzGerald, was absorbing the full extent of his rebuff by Mrs. Thatcher at the Chequers Summit. It seemed that in two successive days Mrs. Thatcher had buried the Forum report and that Dr. McNamara would bury the Taoiseach's constitutional crusade.

This was the public McNamara that the Dublin priests had also indicated their preference against. But from Killarney the other McNamara candidly acknowledged the disappointment of Dublin priests, admitted his own unworthiness for the job and made it clear that he was accepting the office only because he had been asked to do so by the Pope. Public sympathy swung his way. Clerical opposition vanished.

There was apprehension in government circles about how Dr. McNamara would act as "the ecclesiastical Taoiseach" of the Republic. Within the Catholic Church there was anticipation that he would be more like Dr. McQuaid in style than his predecessor, Dr. Ryan. For all his liberal credentials, Dr. Ryan was heavyhanded with his clergy; for all his authoritarian views, Dr. McQuaid was renowned for his pastoral compassion. He was a strong believer in the parish as the local embodiment of the universal Church.

With his highly developed sense of vocation, Dr. McNamara took office in Dublin at a critical stage in Church-State relations. Although he was not known to voice political preferences, his current thinking on the set of issues relating to law, morals and the family, disposes him against the Coalition Government.

One of his early official visits as Archbishop was a call on Dr. FitzGerald at Government Buildings. It was the day before the publication of the government's bill to liberalise contraceptives. The Taoiseach, considering this to be a State matter, neither sought the Archbishop's opinion nor gave him advance notice of its publication. The trial of strength had begun.

Chapter 7

CONTRACEPTION: ROUND TWO

For the first time since the foundation of the Irish State in 1922 the Catholic hierarchy was defeated in a trial of strength with an elected government on a matter of public morality. This historic rebuff of the bishops came when the Dáil passed a Family Planning (Amendment) Bill by a narrow margin on February 20 1985. The Bill's safe passage was immediately welcomed by Dr. FitzGerald as establishing the authority of the State against any form of outside pressure. The northern loyalist newspaper *The Belfast Newsletter* translated this into a bold head-line announcing "Garret beats the bishops".

There had been no doubt in anyone's mind that Church and State were locked into a public debate on the question of sovereignty in the sphere of morality. This became clear as soon as the government announced its proposal to make condoms and spermicides available without a medical prescription to persons aged eighteen and over. Within an hour of the bill's publication the recently appointed Archbishop of Dublin, Dr. Kevin McNamara, denounced it, contending that Ireland was at a moral crossroads and that if the bill were adopted, its "bitter fruits" would be the spread of premarital sex, moral decline, venereal disease, teenage pregnancies, illegitimate births and abortions. He could neither stand aside nor remain silent at the prospect of contraceptives being made legally available to unmarried young people.

Dr. McNamara's opposition took no one by surprise. What did surprise was the speed with which Dr. McNamara reacted and the directness of his attack, as if Ireland was a Garden of Eden when instead the nation had been rocked by a series of extraordinary incidents, in the midlands (where a school-girl, Ann Lovat, died giving birth to a child alone at a grotto) in county Wexford, the case of school-teacher, Eileen Flynn and above all the Joanne Hayes case in Kerry (where a tribunal was in marathon session trying to ascertain the facts about the discovery of two dead babies).

Aware in advance of a possible hostile response from the bishops, the government argued that the bill was a much needed amendment to the 1979 Family Planning Act, which allowed contraceptives to be sold in chemist shops provided that the purchaser furnished a prescription from a doctor. The doctor had to be satisfied that the application for a prescription was for bona fide family planning purposes.

As "an Irish solution to an Irish problem", the 1979 Act made the Irish Republic the only state in the world with legislation governing the sale of non-medical contraceptives. It was recognised that the Act's intention that condoms should be used only for bona fide family planning purposes would be unenforceable in practice. A government review of the Act showed that only a quarter of the nation's chemists were prepared to stock contraceptives and that doctors objected to the statutory task of writing prescriptions for condoms. This review also showed that since the adoption of the Act thirty million condoms had been imported into the State, being sold mainly at family planning clinics without prescription.

The inadequacies of the law were admitted in 1984 by its architect, the former Health Minister, Mr. Charles Haughey. It was one thing for Mr. Haughey to acknowledge the need for a review; it was a different matter when the government proposed a specific amendment. As leader of Fianna Fáil, the largest political party, Mr. Haughey opposed the bill. Thus the government was confronted with the combined opposition of Fianna Fáil, the hierarchy, pulpit priests and lay pressure groups representing the Irish version of America's new moral majority.

Dr. McNamara's swift intervention was followed by action by the conservative lay lobby which put intense pressure on deputies, through phone calls, letters and direct personal solicitation, about the duty of legislators to save Ireland from moral decline; the message to the politicians was that the youth of Ireland must not be encouraged to indulge in sexual permissiveness.

Many bishops felt it necessary to speak out against the bill but most of those who did so observed the policy guideline that had been enunciated several times by the hierarchy as a body in the 1970s: that it was the duty of the politicians to legislate but that the bishops had the right to preach to their flock about the moral impact of a specific piece of proposed legislation. The most notable formulation of this policy had been made only a year earlier to the New Ireland Forum when Bishop Cahal Daly of Belfast renounced any wish for a Catholic State for a Catholic people.

During the public debate on the bill, the episcopal contributor who stuck closest to the guidelines was Bishop Brendan Comiskey of Ferns, who had topped the private poll among the Dublin clergy for the succession to the late Archbishop Ryan. In an address in Wexford Dr. Comiskey said that, since 1973 the bishops had repeatedly made it clear that it was for legislators to legislate, that was not the function of bishops. But as teachers and pastors, bishops had a duty to alert the consciences of Catholics to the moral consequences of proposed legislation and to the effect it would be likely to have on society.

There was only one official contribution to the debate in the name of all the bishops and that came from the spokesman, Bishop Cassidy of Clonfert, who repeated the 1973 guidelines and said that the Episcopal Conference had not changed its position since the Forum. While the statements of Archbishop McNamara and Bishop Newman strained Dr. Cassidy's assertion, what counts for the record is the collective pronouncement, not the declarations of individual bishops. The hierarchy as a whole had not issued a statement because it had had no time to react.

The 1973 guidelines were not fully adhered to by Dr. McNamara and by Dr. Newman of Limerick, neither of whom had attended the Forum. Criticising *a la carte* Catholicism, Dr. McNamara argued that politicians could not separate their Catholic beliefs from their political responsibilities and he told them that they must act on behalf of the common good. Even more bluntly, Dr. Newman advised the politicians that they must follow the guidelines of their bishops and he urged Catholic citizens to use their clout.

Dr. FitzGerald and his ministers were surprised that Dr. McNamara and Dr. Newman did not adhere to the Forum

91

pronouncement on the respective duties and obligations of politicians. Such ecclesiastical crozier-waving put the condom debate onto the level of a major Church-State confrontation. The outcome of the voting was in doubt until the last moment. Although three Fine Gael deputies voted against (Alice Glenn, Tom O'Donnell and Oliver J. Flanagan), and one Labour deputy, Sean Treacy, opposed, the bill was carried with the support of the two members of the Workers Party, Tomás MacGiolla and Proinsias de Rossa and that of the Independent Dublin deputy, Mr. Tony Gregory.

The outcome had repercussions on the political composition of Dáil Éireann. The three Fine Gael deputies lost the party whip, though this rupture was healed without fuss later in the year. Mr. Sean Treacy broke his connection with Labour and became an Independent. But the biggest change involved the deputy who had made the most acclaimed speech in the debate, Mr. Desmond O'Malley, Mr. Haughey's arch rival for the leadership of Fianna Fáil. The previous year Mr. O'Malley had lost the Fianna Fáil party whip for publicly taking a broader view of the New Ireland Forum options than the united Ireland solution stipulated by Mr. Haughey as the only option.

In his "I stand by the Republic" speech to the Dáil, Mr. O,Malley warned that if the condom bill were defeated the two elements who would rejoice to high heaven would be the unionists in Northern Ireland and the extremist Roman Catholics in the Republic. He reminded the house that the republican tradition aimed to reconcile Catholic, Protestant and Dissenter, not to pass restrictive legislation that was contrary to the conscience of individuals. In response to Drs. McNamara and Newman, Mr. O'Malley quoted New York State governor, Mario Cuomo:

"Catholics must practise the teachings of Christ, not just by trying to make laws for others to live by but by living the laws already written for us by God. We can be fully Catholic, clearly, proudly, totally at ease with ourselves, a people in the world transforming it, a light to this nation, appealing to the best in our people, not to the worst. Leading people to truth by love and still all the while respecting and enjoying our unique pluralistic democracy and we can do it as politicians".

Mr. O'Malley soon paid a political price for daring to recommend that pluralism might be good for Ireland. Although he said he would abstain, he was not present in the house when the vote was taken. Within days the national executive met and expelled Mr. O'Malley from the Fianna Fáil party. Ten months later Mr. O'Malley launched a new political party, the Progressive Democrats, which aims to end the Civil War mould of Irish politics and to separate Church and State in the Republic.

From a northern perspective Barry White of *The Belfast Telegraph* saw the most striking aspect of the contraceptive debate as the total lack of consideration for the effects on the political situation in the North or on the possibility of Dr. FitzGerald securing, in the continuing negotiations with Mrs. Thatcher, a role for the Republic in the running of Northern Ireland. The SDLP leader, John Hume, whose strategy at the Forum had been based on an accommodation of differences, north and south, was embarrassed, while unionists are rubbing their hands with glee, delighted that the British and foreign media are getting a grandstand view of the Catholic Church fighting to preserve the Catholicism of the Republic, regardless of the Protestant North".

The acclaimed hero of the confrontation was the Minister for Health, Barry Desmond, who appeared to revel under pressure while professing simply to be doing his day's work. "I am an elected member of a sovereign government. Because of the office I hold with responsibility for health and welfare", he told journalists at Leinster House, "I have to legislate for all. I regard the issue as a health matter. I don't regard it as a confrontationary matter with any Church".

Although the outcome enabled Dr. FitzGerald to restore some of the prestige which he had lost during the anti-abortion campaign, he received little comfort from this victory when reaction from the party's grass-roots to the passage of the bill proved hostile.

Pronouncing his verdict on the confrontation Dr. John Whyte wrote that "if all the bishops had spoken in the same terms as Dr. Cassidy and Dr. Comiskey, there would have been no opportunity to describe Mr. Desmond's Act as a defeat for the Church - any more than Mr. Haughey's Act of

1979 could be described in such terms. It was the statements of Dr. McNamara and Dr. Newman which turned the episode into a confrontation in which one side or the other was bound to appear as a victor. Since they lost, the Church appeared to have suffered its most clear cut defeat since the establishment of the State''.

Chapter 8

CARDINAL CASAROLI IN DUBLIN

"It cannot be denied that during the fifty years which followed the establishment of an independent Irish State, there was a considerable intimacy between the State and the Catholic Church. The extent of this intimacy has been greatly exaggerated in some quarters, and in many ways the close relationship which marked that period was quite understandable, given the prevailing historical factors and the overwhelming proportion of Catholics in the population".

This candid assessment of Church-State relations between 1922 and 1972 was made by the Minister for Foreign Affairs, Mr Peter Barry, in the course of a major speech which he delivered on Monday September 16th 1985 at a luncheon in Iveagh House. It was a carefully prepared speech, one which Mr Barry delivered word for word from his text. His caution was understandable. In the presence of important guests he was making sure that they knew his remarks were carefully chosen.

Seated on his left was a fellow Corkman, Monsignor Patrick Coveney, a diplomat in the service of the Holy See, who, the previous day in his home-town had been raised to the rank of Apostolic Pro-Nuncio to Zimbabwe and Apostolic Delegate to Mozambique. Across the table were Cardinal Tomás Ó Fiaich and the Apostolic Nuncio to Ireland, Archbishop Gaetano Alibrandi. Most importantly, on Mr Barry's right was the guest of honour, Agostino Casaroli, now the Vatican Cardinal Secretary of State, a position which makes him the Pope's 'Prime Minister'.

Seated at other tables were representatives of Church and State. These included three archbishops, Dr Kevin McNamara, Dr Joseph Cunnane and Dr Thomas Morris; Bishops Gerard Brooks of Dromore, Eamonn Casey of Galway, Joseph Duffy of Clogher, Michael Harty of Killaloe, Patrick

Lennon of Kildare and Leighlin, Francis McKiernan of Kilmore, Jeremiah Newman of Limerick; the President of Maynooth College, Father Michael Ledwith, Monsignor Padilla of Opus Dei, Deputy Oliver J. Flanagan, a Knight of the Order of St Gregory and a member of the Knights of St Columbanus. Among the politicians were former Taoisigh Jack Lynch and Liam Cosgrave; the deputy leader of Fianna Fáil, Brian Lenihan, and two Senators, John Robb and Bríd Rogers.

The guests had one thing in common: they were curious to observe keenly the mannerisms of a speaker and to interpret the diplomatic nuances of a speech.

The cordial formalities were observed scrupulously by Mr Barry: a generous tribute to Cardinal Casaroli for his enormous work for peace and reconciliation which had made him "something of a legend in the field of diplomacy", appreciation of Archbishop Coveney's promotion; regret at the sudden death in Rome of Dr Dermot Ryan. Mr Barry also praised the work of Irish missionaries and the Catholic Church's contribution in Ireland since the foundation of the State to educational, health and welfare systems.

The word "intimacy" to describe the Church-State relationship from 1922-1972 signalled to the guests that Mr Barry was nearing the central part of his address.

"In retrospect", Mr Barry continued, "it has been argued - most notably by the Catholic bishops at the Public Session of the New Ireland Forum on February 9th, 1984, - that the alliance of Church and State was harmful - for both parties. That is why the Catholic bishops, to quote one member of the hierarchy, rejoiced when the provision concerning the special position of the Catholic Church was removed from the constitution, following the referendum of 1972".

Mr Barry was now at the heart of his message: "In the period since 1972, a new form of relationship has evolved between the State and the various Churches and religious denominations. Sometimes this has led to instances of misunderstanding. Measured against international standards, the causes of these difficulties have been minor, but in an Irish context they have occasionally been allowed to assume major proportions". The Minister did not need to spell out to his listeners that he was referring to the 1983 anti-abortion referendum and to the passage through the Dáil a few months earlier of the law liberalising the sale of contraceptives. Nor did he mention by name the looming battle - the major trial of strength - over divorce.

Such difficulties were "a source of regret to the government, not least because little or no benefit accrues to either the Churches or the State when they are seen to be at loggerheads. The government accepts, however, that these episodes are the price that has to be paid for a relationship with the Churches that is based on equality and mutual respect.

"As the Government sees it, there are two basic principles involved in this relationship. These appear to have been publicly accepted by the representatives of the Catholic Church at the New Ireland Forum. Firstly, every Church and religious denomination has, subject to the provisions of the constitution, the right to speak out on any issue they wish. Particular recognition is given to the duty of Church leaders to alert the consciences of their followers to what they perceive to be the moral consequences of any proposed legislation, or its effect on the moral quality of life in society.

"Secondly, the members of the Oireachtas have the right, based on the democratic principles reflected in the constitution, to legislate in accordance with their conscience, in what they consider to be the best interests of the Irish people. These, I repeat, are principles recognised by representatives of the Catholic hierarchy at the New Ireland Forum. They would seem to represent a sound basis for relations between the State and all Churches and denominations.

"If, as may happen, the legislators don't follow the advice of one, or even any, of the Churches, it is important for everyone involved to keep any such disagreement in perspective. We must be prepared to compare the situation in Ireland with that pertaining elsewhere. We must set any problems against the ongoing record of close cooperation between the State and the Churches in many spheres of Irish life".

The Anglo-Irish negotiations formed the theme of the final section of Mr Barry's speech. Recalling the appeal made by Pope John Paul II in Drogheda in 1979 when, on his knees, he begged the men of violence to turn away from the path of violence, Mr Barry said that lasting peace and stability had not yet been achieved in Northern Ireland but that this was the goal in the talks between Dr FitzGerald and Mrs Thatcher. "Acknowledgements of the need for new structures and processes which would accommodate the rights and identities of the unionist and nationalist communities have been made by both governments", he said. "If an agreement were reached, it would be worthy of the support of the vast majority of the people of the island of Ireland. In such circumstances, support of Church leaders for the peace process would be of very great importance".

Cardinal Casaroli replied with a bland speech which threw no light on either the Vatican's official response to Mr Barry's definition of the basis for the conduct of Church-State relations or to his appeal for church support for the Anglo-Irish peace process. But diplomatic sources suggested afterwards that the Cardinal had understood - and had not been put out by - Mr Barry's message. In April 1984 Mr Barry had been received at the Vatican by Cardinal Casaroli. In their talks on Northern Ireland which were also attended by the secretary of the Council of Public Affairs, Archbishop Achille Silvestrini, Mr Barry informed them of the Irish Government's concern at the deterioration of the situation in the north and of the urgent need for the Irish and British governments to launch a peace initiative.

On that visit Mr Barry had an audience with Pope John Paul at which, contrary to advance speculation, he did not raise the issue of Vatican policy on mixed marriages. Mr Barry had decided that it would be "inappropriate" to raise the question. Incidentally, in the April 1984 issue of *Doctrine and Life* Mrs Una O'Higgins-O'Malley, a daughter of Kevin O'Higgins, the government minister assassinated in 1927, had a private audience with the Pope. She was accompanied by a Belfast Protestant woman. They put before the Pope their views on the problems of Northern Ireland and on how the Catholic Church might contribute to their solution through a relaxation of the mixed marriage rules.

John Paul's concern for a break-through in the Anglo-Irish talks was indicated in June 1985 when he received the credentials of the new British Ambassador to the Holy See, Mr David Lane. The Pope's encouragement to the Ambassasdor to encourage and support "every worthy effort" to solve the Irish question was interpreted as a diplomatic triumph for the Dublin government.

While in Dublin, Cardinal Casaroli had a private meeting with Dr FitzGerald. The exclusion of the nuncio fuelled further press speculation about Dr Alibrandi's relations with the government. We do not know what was said between the Taoiseach and the Cardinal. We can assume it was an opportunity for them to catch up on events since Dr FitzGerald's 1977 visit to the Vatican.

We can assume too that Cardinal Casaroli, the diplomat of *realpolitik* who had to deal with Communist, anti-clerical and secular governments, was less agitated than the Irish hierarchy about the reforms of the FitzGerald government. He had shown more than passive interest in Dr FitzGerald's proposals in the 1970s. Otherwise why would he have arranged access for him to Pope Paul VI and to Archbishop Benelli? Whatever may have been possible in 1977 was out of reach in 1985. There was no way that Pope John Paul would contemplate non-resistance by the Irish bishops to the introduction of divorce. The architect of Paul VI's *ostpolitik* could not deliver on FitzGerald's *nordpolitik*.

Chapter 9

DIVORCE

At a lunch in Government Buildings on Monday 12 May 1986, for political correspondents, Dr. Garret FitzGerald was in a relaxed mood. He had the air of a man who was relieved to have made a major decision and, win or lose, was prepared to live with the consequences of what he believed was a correct decision. This was the decision taken by the goverment on 23 April to hold a referendum in June to remove the constitutional ban on divorce and to insert into the constitution a provision permitting divorce for couples whose marriages had failed for at least five years. Divorces would be granted by new family courts only if there was no possibility of a reconciliation of the couple and after mediation had failed.

An early *Irish Times/MRBI* opinion poll showed that 57 per cent favoured the government's limited divorce proposal, 36 per cent were opposed to it, and only seven per cent were undecided.

The Fianna Fáil parliamentary party decided not to oppose the bill's passage in the Dáil and not to campaign in the referendum as a party, leaving it up to the individual deputies and senators to act according to conscience. An interim response from the four Catholic archbishops described the bill as providing the basis for the most unrestrictive form of divorce in the world.

At the lunch Dr. FitzGerald felt that the campaign would begin in the most favourable circumstance possible for the government. But that evening in Longford the Minister for Education, Mr. Patrick Cooney, repeated his objections to divorce at a party meeting and reportedly said that it would be daft to vote for divorce. Next day Fine Gael backbencher, Oliver Flanagan, appealed to "the silent majority" to oppose the measure from the "anti-family wing of the government". The gloves were off.

On Wednesday 14 May *The Irish Times* published the details of a new offensive by the Catholic bishops against divorce. It reported that one million copies of a new pastoral, *Marriage, the Family and Divorce,* were to be published and distributed nationwide. This letter, largely an abridged and popular form of the bulkier 1985 letter, *Love is for Life,* rejected the government's view that a divorce law "in a country like Ireland will be minimal in effect". Divorce, the bishops argued, would immediately define all marriages as dissoluble rather than being for life.

News of the extent of the bishops' involvement in influencing the outcome of the referendum at the ballot box had a dramatic effect on the politicians as they began that morning in the Dáil the historic debate on the government's divorce bill. As the Taoiseach moved quickly at a Fine Gael parliamentary party meeting to minimise the damage done to party unity, it became clear that Fianna Fáil deputies were using arguments and language which echoed closely those used by the bishops. The tone was set when the Fianna Fáil spokesman, Michael Woods, argued that a divorce law would not simply affect those who had suffered marital breakdown but would apply to every citizen. Like the Catholic bishops, Dr. Woods invoked the spectre of a constitutional frankenstein stalking the land if divorce were introduced.

The passage of the bill through the Dáil took place therefore against the background of divisions across the main political parties about the morality of divorce, and of a campaign by some bishops and clergy to defeat the measure. Referendum day, Thursday 26 June was therefore to be the decisive day in the unfolding battle between the Catholic Church and the State. It was a day which would be the culmination of a complex process of consultation and preparation since late 1982.

The Joint Committee on Marriage Breakdown

Dr. FitzGerald had begun his second administration in November 1982 in partnership with Labour, whose leader was now Dick Spring. The 30 page programme for government devoted only three paragraphs to what was euphemistically called "social reforms". The third specifically promised:

"The reform of the marriage laws will be examined by a Committee of the Oireachtas before the end of 1983, which will recommend on the problems of the protection of marriage under modern conditions and of marriage breakdown and on any legislative or constitutional action that may be required".

This timetable was not kept, because of the preoccupation by the nation with what Gene Kerrigan in *Magill* magazine described as "the moral civil war" - the anti-abortion amendment campaign. It was not until July 1983 that the committee's membership was announced. But the committee did not hold its first meeting until 14 September, a week after the conclusion of the pro-life amendment. An exhausted and divided society had little chance to recover from its bruises before the divorce battlelines were being drawn-up.

On the morning of the referendum results Olivia O'Leary reported in *The Irish Times* that Fianna Fáil might rethink its opposition to divorce on account of a growing public perception that Fianna Fáil had become conservative. Aware of the label "the bishops' party", strategists were concerned at the rejection of the pro-life amendment in five Dublin area constituencies. The deputy leader, Mr. Lenihan, was reported to have indicated to officials that policy on marriage breakdown would be reviewed. This was to lead to Mr. Haughey's decision in April 1986 not to oppose the divorce referendum bill in the Dáil and to allow deputies freedom of conscience in the campaign.

The possibility of a more flexible Fianna Fáil approach appeared to augur well for the work of the new committee, at whose inaugural meeting no one mentioned a seven letter word beginning with D and ending with E. Its chairman was the veteran East Limerick Fine Gael deputy, Willie O'Brien, who acquired a deservedly good reputation for patient steering of an often rowdy crew. Most vocal were the lawyer-politicians, among them Alan Shatter, and Senators Mary Robinson, Catherine McGuinness and Katherine Bulbulia.

The Fianna Fáil membership consisted of former Health Minister, Michael Woods, the flamboyant Mayo West deputy, Pádraig Flynn, the Galway West deputy, Máire Geoghegan-Quinn, its Health front-bench spokesman, Dr. Rory O'Hanlon from Monaghan, and Mary Harney, who was later to be a founder member of the Progressive Democrats, and Senators Tom Hussey and Treas Honan. Other Fine Gael members were the Cork deputy, Myra Barry, Dick Dowling, Carlow-Kilkenny, and Madeline Taylor-Quinn of Clare. Labour was represented by former Health Minister, Eileen Desmond.

Like any good committee, it decided to tackle the most difficult problem - divorce - last. After an initial burst of publicity, the committee settled down to making sense of the country's marriage muddle. Journalist Don Buckley reported in *The Irish Independent* that "conservative members of the committee, particularly some of the Fianna Fáil representatives, who may not have realised the full extent of marriage breakdown have had their eyes opened by the flood of submissions when evidence was invited from the public". Most of these submissions, he added, were sad accounts of broken marriages and their consequences. About 90 per cent favoured divorce. Over thirty letters detailing separate marriage breakdowns came from one small parish alone.

A big problem for the marriage committee was ascertaining the extent of marriage breakdown. With no reliable official figures - this would not be rectified until the publication of the 1986 census which specifically dealt with marriage breakdowns - it was difficult to state the precise number of failed marriages. The 1983 Labour Force Survey estimated that 8,300 married males and 12,800 married females were separated, giving a total of 21,100 persons.

The Divorce Action Group, however, argued that the figures were far higher, affecting in excess of 70,000 persons including children. These figures were contested in December 1983 by the Bishop of Kerry, Dr. McNamara, who accused the divorce lobby of tossing about figures which were of pure conjecture.

The committee needed four extensions to complete its work. Leaks indicated that the committee was faced with a strong reaction from Fianna Fáil members against any commitment on the introduction of divorce. Even before the report was published, it was clear that it would receive a critical, if not hostile media response. An *Irish Times* editorial on 15 March 1985 ridiculed the committee for failing "to find an

Irish, or any, solution to an Irish problem". While recommending a referendum to remove the constitutional ban, the committee made no proposal about the kind of divorce law which would be appropriate.

The report appeared on 2 April 1985. Because of the compromise on the divorce question, the report's merits were not fully appreciated by the media. It dealt with education and counselling services, and with the legal remedies available to those whose marriages have broken down, including the law of nullity, legal and judicial separation, maintenance, guardianship and custody, matrimonial property and barring orders. It also proposed the establishment of Family Tribunals.

Rather than the publication of the report marking the start of a new phase of vigorous decision-making by the government, the divorce debate entered a period of all-round muddle. Dr. FitzGerald resisted suggestions to proceed with divorce legislation, arguing that the report - which he considered to be a good one - needed to be debated in the Dáil and the Senate. But the Anglo-Irish negotiations on Northern Ireland were taking longer than anticipated. On the economic front the government's popularity had slumped since August 1984 when food subsidies were abolished. Dr. FitzGerald was in no rush towards a divorce referendum. It was not until late June that the committee's report was presented for debate in the Senate - only to be adjourned - until September.

Meanwhile, the Catholic bishops, claiming to have been taken unawares by the government on the liberalisation of the contraceptive law, were mounting an advance campaign against divorce. A pastoral letter, *Love is for Life,* was read out in churches throughout the country on three successive Sundays in March. "No legislative enactment can dissolve a valid marriage", the four archbishops wrote, "and leave the partner free to marry again. Remarriage of a civilly divorced person is not a real marriage in the sight of God".

This pulpit offensive appeared to backfire in Dublin where many priests shared the *ennui* of the laity, but elsewhere in the country the opinion polls showed an increase in the numbers against removing the divorce ban. Archbishop McNamara also addressed Family Solidarity, one of the staunchest anti-divorce groups, on the subject of "Pluralism: unravelling a riddle of our time".

Nor did the coldest and wettest summer in living memory dispose the politicians to action on divorce. Instead, attention focused on "moving statues" at Ballinspittle, County Cork, and other shrines. Crowds flocked to remote Culleens in County Sligo where the Virgin Mary was reported to have appeared to schoolgirls. Faced with such a resurgence of devotionalism in Irish Catholicism, the politicians detected a holy-water trend which was inimical to constitutional crusaders. It became conventional wisdom among politicians and commentators that the government had shelved any plans for holding a divorce referendum within its lifetime. This was especially so after the June local elections resulted in Fianna Fáil's regaining of ground lost in 1979. In August Dick Spring admitted that he felt a certain frustration on the divorce issue. Both Mr. Spring and the Congress of Trades Unions called for a campaign to educate public opinion on the need for divorce legislation. But the strength of the political tide in Fianna Fáil's favour was seen on 1 September when the *Sunday Independent* published an *Irish Marketing Surveys* opinion poll giving Fianna Fáil an 18 per cent lead over Fine Gael and Labour. The state of the parties was Fine Gael, 30 per cent; Labour, 7 per cent; Fianna Fáil, 55 per cent.

In an *Irish Times* interview on 24 September Mr. Barry said that the Taoiseach's constitutional crusade was still alive but that it had been put to one side while the Anglo-Irish negotiations were still going on. The Minister also said he was unaware of any government undertaking to hold a referendum to remove the divorce prohibition. There had been no discussion of it by the government, and he did not know how soon consideration would be given to such a referendum. No decision would be taken until the report of the Joint Committee had been debated.

Mr. Barry's remarks dismayed the Divorce Action Group, which had organised a press conference in Buswell's Hotel to rally support on the eve of the resumed Senate debate on the Joint Report. At this news conference Senator Mary Robinson threatened to defy a Labour three-line whip to vote with Fine Gael colleagues against a motion from Independent

105

Senators Shane Ross and Brendan Ryan calling for a divorce referendum to be held within the Government's lifetime.

At this time too the annual meeting of the National Conference of Priests of Ireland was taking place at Swords, Co. Dublin, at which concern was expressed that the credibility of the Catholic Church might suffer if there was another confrontation with the State over divorce. While upholding the Church's right and duty to press its views on public morality, it was also stressed that the lessons of the 1983 referendum campaign must be learned. At a briefing session for reporters Father Austin Flannery OP, the editor of *Doctrine and Life,* said that there was a feeling among the priests that "there should be no secret lobbying and no demagoguery, if the divorce issue comes before the people".

This appeal from the priests was welcomed by Senator Katherine Bulbulia in the Senate debate on the Joint Committee's report, but she regretted that statements by Bishop Newman of Limerick attempted to undermine legislators and by extension to undermine democracy. She was referring to a new Church-State controversy between Bishop Newman and the Minister for Agriculture, Mr. Austin Deasy, arising from the luncheon in honour of Cardinal Casaroli. Bishop Newman, who had been among the bishops present at the luncheon in Iveagh House, complained afterwards that Mr. Barry had delivered "a lecture". The bishop also declared that "politicians who profess to be Catholics are not entitled to follow their consciences in a void, as if a teaching authority did not exist in the Catholic Church". In reply, Mr. Deasy upheld the government's independence of action in legislative matters and told the bishop that ministers were doing their job without challenging or consulting the interests of any religious group.

In the resumed senate debate Mr. Michael D Higgins said that without the promise of a referendum it would be easier for prominent public figures such as Archbishop McNamara to trample even more on "a significant development in modern theology - the acceptance of the notion of an informed conscience". Mr. Higgins also attacked "authoritarian, bullying statements by those who claim to speak from a higher

106

level". He accused Dr. McNamara of not having the courage to say "we want legislators to pass the Catholic legislation".

Senator Pat Magner, Labour, calling for a referendum, said that banning divorce was like banning funerals to prevent death. The Fianna Fáil leader in the Senate, Mr. Michael Lanigan, said it was quite obvious that the government had no intention of holding a referendum, and he regretted that the emphasis in the debate had not been on the protection of family life rather than on marital breakdown. Senator Charlie McDonald, Fine Gael, urged the State to recognise Catholic Church annulments, and appealed to those opposed to divorce to consider the position of broken marriages from a more humane point of view.

The Senate debate ended on 6 November in uproar, with a procedural row. Fianna Fáil abstained in the vote. The amendment, tabled by Senators Ryan and Ross for the holding of a referendum within the lifetime of the government, was defeated by 20 votes to 14.

Meanwhile Archbishop McNamara had re-entered the debate on Saturday 29 September when he addressed the annual meeting of The Knights of St Columbanus at Malahide, Co. Dublin. The Archbishop warned Catholic politicians not to dismiss the guidance offered by the bishops on moral issues, advice which was directed at no specific politician but which was clearly a rebuke to Mr Barry for his Casaroli luncheon address on the separate functions of Church and State. Dr McNamara also expressed total opposition to the introduction of civil divorce in the Republic. The response of the Knights, the biggest Catholic men's organisation in Ireland, was to pass a resolution in private session calling for clear leadership from the Catholic Church authorities on matters of faith and morals.

Enter Michael O'Leary

The headlines in the *Sunday Tribune* next morning went not to Dr McNamara but to a politician who had enjoyed many headlines as a minister, as Tánaiste and as leader of the Labour party but who had gone out of the news since his controversial move to the Fine Gael back-benches, Michael O'Leary. Political Correspondent, Gerry Barry, reported

107

that Mr O'Leary had prepared two bills - one to delete the divorce ban from the constitution and the second detailing how divorce would be allowed in certain circumstances. "The most novel aspect of Mr O'Leary's draft bills is that they would allow the electorate not just the right to delete the present constitutional ban on divorce, but would allow the voters themselves the final right to reject or accept any changes in laws affecting marriage. Each proposed change would be put in a referendum of the full electorate", he wrote.

Gerry Barry also reported that in the second of the two bills, which would have to be endorsed by the electorate as well as by the houses of the Oireachtas, Mr O'Leary proposed:

- A system of separation orders which could be granted by the High Court on grounds of adultery, physical or mental cruelty, or unreasonable behaviour.
- Separation where both parties have lived apart for at least one year and where both consent to the separation order.
- Dissolution of marriage on grounds of irretrievable breakdown after two years' separation where both parties consent or after five years living apart where only one partner wants the marriage to be dissolved.
- The right of all couples, whose marriages have been dissolved, to re-marry.
- All children of dissolved marriages would continue to be the lawful child of each of the parties of the original marriage.

The Sunday Tribune stated that while the Joint Committee failed at the final hurdle, Mr O'Leary was offering the legislature a real opportunity to "face the reality of a problem which has already increased dramatically and is likely to lead to even greater misery and hardship in the years ahead". As far back as April Mr O'Leary had served notice of his own intention of bringing forward proposals if the delay in dealing with divorce persisted.

Mr O'Leary's initiative was greeted with cynicism by his colleagues in Fine Gael and his former colleagues in Labour. While Fine Gael agreed that there should be a free vote, not even the liberal wing of the party felt Mr O'Leary's bills worth supporting. The Labour party, embarrassed by its inaction, instructed its chief whip, Mervyn Taylor and Senator Mary Robinson to bring forward their own bill.

Another important effect of Mr O'Leary's intervention was that on a *Today Tonight* interview Dr FitzGerald for the first time publicly said that he would like to see the ban on divorce removed from the constitution. Interestingly, too, Mr O'Leary sent copies of his bills to Church leaders. From Dr McNamara he received a copy of *Love is for Life*.

On 5 November Mr O'Leary's bills failed to secure a second reading. They were supported by only four deputies, Mr Tómas MacGiolla and Mr Proinsías de Rossa of the Workers Party, Mr Tony Gregory, Independent, and Fine Gael backbencher, Mr Liam Skelly. With the defeat of these bills, the Labour party formally placed its bill on the order paper but did not move it. The next move was the ordering of the debate on the report by the Joint Committee. At Question Time Dr FitzGerald told the Dáil that no decision about a divorce referendum would be taken by the government until the committee's report had been given full consideration.

The Dáil Debate

"I ask all members not to allow this debate to become a farce. I do not want to hear set speeches whose sole purpose is to support a party line ... I should like this house to treat this major social issue with the respect it deserves".

So pleaded Mr Willie O'Brien, when he opened the long delayed Dáil debate on the Joint Committee's report on Thursday 14 November, the day before Dr FitzGerald signed the Anglo-Irish Agreement with the British Prime Minister, Mrs Margaret Thatcher, in Hillsborough, Co. Down.

On Friday 24 January at 10.05 pm what had been billed as the start of the national debate on marriage and divorce by the legislators petered out not in farce, not in party cant, though its five scattered sessions contained elements of both, but in self-induced silence: no one else wanted to speak. Only 35 out of 165 deputies - or roughly one in five - had taken part in the debate which was frequently held up because the quorum of twenty deputies was not met. At one point the Fine Gael deputy for Dublin South, Alan Shatter, sat in the seat of the leader of the Opposition to draw attention to the absence of all the Fianna Fáil members.

Of those who spoke - 19 from Fine Gael, 12 from Fianna Fáil, 3 from Labour and Mr Proinsías de Rossa of the Workers Party - the contributions were of a high standard, were sincere and were presented with conviction. Their comments reflected the deep divisions within society on divorce, as was summed up by Mr O'Brien when he said "there were compelling arguments for divorce but there were equally convincing arguments against it".

The standard Fianna Fáil argument was put by the party's spokesman on Health, Dr Rory O'Hanlon, when he said that it was for the government to decide whether to hold a referendum. Not convinced that divorce was in the interests of society, Dr O'Hanlon urged that improvements could be made in areas such as education in relationships, better marriage preparation and counselling and in nullity. This argument was given doctrinaire pugnancy by West Mayo deputy, Pádraig Flynn, whose contribution was described later by Dick Dowling of Fine Gael as having put the gloss on the anti-divorce submission from the Knock Marriage Bureau in perhaps the greatest defence of the existing situation that anybody could deliver in the house.

But Mr Flynn's argument did not convince Mr Dowling who, though personally against divorce, said that "if I could be guaranteed, if we brought in a form of divorce by making a constitutional amendment, that irretrievable marriage breakdown only would be the ground for divorce, I would be reasonably happy".

Fianna Fáil speakers were doubtful of the need of divorce: Pádraig Faulkner, Louth, felt that the cure (of divorce) would become worse than the disease; Mary O'Rourke, Longford-Westmeath, though favouring a referendum, did not see how a limited divorce law could be implemented without becoming more extensive. Denis Foley, Kerry North, said divorce was not the answer to marriage problems and it was not in the best interests of society; Michael Barrett, Dublin North-West, agreed with his colleague Michael Woods that he would be happy if the government chose to hold a referendum, but the wording of such a resolution "would have to be examined in great detail by our leader, our parliamentary party and our front-bench before we could agree to it". Chief Whip, Vincent Brady, confessed that he had not come across, or experienced, the huge demand that was alleged to be there for divorce. Fianna Fáil had a duty and a responsibility to ensure that the government would not be rushed into changing the whole fabric of society. Mr Michael O'Kennedy did not deal with divorce but associated himself with those who opposed control or direction from any Church.

Dr John O'Connell, recalling that 16 years earlier he was branded as a dangerous liberal for initiating a public debate on divorce, described the present situation as intolerable. But he did not think "we should proceed headlong with legislation allowing divorce without a proper public debate and without examining divorce laws in other countries and their defects. Mr Charlie McCreevy, Kildare, referred to his own marital problems and said he had always believed the constitutional ban on divorce to be wrong. He also suggested that there should be no party whip imposed on the issue.

Mr David Andrews, Fianna Fáil, said "in almost every civilised state in the world divorce is a recognised human right and there is no evidence of which I am aware that, in Catholic countries where divorce is available, the principle that marriage is a lifelong commitment has been seriously breached"; the Dail should recognise that "for some people at some stage divorce is inevitable".

The three Labour speakers were pro-referendum and pro-divorce. The Minister for Health, Mr Barry Desmond, said "what we are talking about when we visualise the possibility of divorce is not - I would stress - the severance of a deep emotional bond or the destruction of a happy family, but the ending, in a purely legalistic sense, of a relationship which has become a mere formality". He also invoked the Anglo-Irish Agreement, asking "how do we expect to convince the unionists that there is benefit to them in this accord while refusing to move one inch to meet them on issues such as divorce?"

Mr Mervyn Taylor, chief whip, said "The introduction of divorce legislation would bring about a tremendous transformation in the lives of the many couples and their children who

111

are suffering because of marital breakdown. It would give these couples a second chance and some hope and comfort for the future".

Mr Michael Bell, Louth, said: "As a practising Catholic I try to live by the Ten Commandments. I do not think they contain anything that says one cannot have divorce or that one cannot remarry. They talk about adultery and many other matters but they do not say anything about being unable to remarry. If one wanted to talk about going to heaven, then if all the people who have been divorced and are happily remarried could not go there, there would be hardly sufficient room for them in hell".

Fine Gael speakers divided broadly into crusaders and defenders. In the former category were Nuala Fennell, Maurice Manning, Liam Skelly, Nora Owen, Alan Shatter, Richard Bruton, George Birmingham, Bernard Allen, Mary Flaherty and Monica Barnes. The defenders were represented by Alice Glenn Paddy Cooney.

A surprise convert to the crusaders from the right wing of Fine Gael was Brendan McGahon, Louth, who said "Although I tend to be conservative by nature I have to confess that on this issue I have liberal views I am not a statistician and I have no figures available. I am using my own gut instinct and my observation of life in my own neck of the woods and know that marital breakdown is very definitely in our midst".

Mr McGahon rivalled his Labour colleague, Michael Bell, in expounding the Louth school of theology. "There is a God of love as well as a God of wrath", Mr McGahon said. "For many generations Irish people have been fed on a diet of the God of wrath. I have enough belief in God, a simple belief, to expect that nobody will be consigned to the dungeons of hell because they failed to make their marriage work. Many churchmen also share that belief."

Bernard Allen, Cork North Central, said "We as politicians should be concerned about the social impact of divorce. We must decide whether divorce will create greater problems while lessening the problems we have at present due to the absence of divorce. We must decide on this issue and each person in the State will have to debate it in his mind in the months ahead. I hope that a referendum will be held to give the people a final say, but we as legislators must legislate for all people in the country irrespective of our religious beliefs".

Mrs Alice Glenn said that divorce, contraception, abortion and alternative life styles taken together took on the appearance of a Trojan horse. The cultural and political arguments about them reflected the deep philosophical chasm between radically opposed visions of our society.

"The struggle is between the Judaeo-Christian ethic based on the God-given tradition of eternal law and the humanist vision which rejects God and traditional values", she said.

Falling into the hesitant crusader category was Cork's Myra Barry, who was anxious to avoid "another bitter, abusive and divisive debate" such as had happened in the anti-abortion amendment. But"one thing I know is that the people are sick of politicians sweeping the issues under the carpet. There are lives involved, childrens' lives, and we cannot put off the evil day forever".

It was Mr de Rossa of the Workers Party who highlighted the limits to the debate. It was not a debate at all but a series of statements. It had also been agreed by the whips that there would be no vote when the talk concluded. "The decision to have the debate in this form indicates what can only be described as an obsessive reluctance by the major parties to avoid confronting the issue of marriage breakdown in a realistic way", he said. "The entire circumstances surrounding the establishment of the Committee and through its life, to the arrangements of this debate, I feel have been characterised by what can only be called political cowardice and opportunism, particularly on the part of the largest party in this house, Fianna Fáil. This is opportunism of the worst kind because it ignores the real pain and anguish that thousands of people must face".

Enter John Hume

Friday 6 December 1985 was notable for two important speeches on divorce, one of them in the Dáil debate, the second at a meeting of the Association of European Journalists at Dublin's Elm Park Golf Club. The first was by the then Defence Minister, Mr Patrick Cooney, who, like Mrs Alice Glenn, welcomed an early referendum, because he was confi-

113

dent that it would be defeated. "I want to say quite clearly that I am in favour of the retention of the constitutional prohibition on divorce, because I consider that the nature of marriage as a lifelong commitment should be retained and should not be changed and transformed into a conditional alliance to be dissolved at the wish of the parties to it". Mr Cooney was confident that the majority of Fine Gael deputies would campaign against any change in the legal code.

Mr Hume accepted the Catholic Church's view that politicians must look at the social consequences of divorce legislation, because divorce did create serious social consequences. "If there is going to be a referendum on divorce in the Republic - and that decision must be taken by the Republic's political parties - people must know precisely what kind of divorce law they are voting on", he stressed.

Asked if the Republic should introduce divorce to please the unionists in Northern Ireland, Mr Hume replied that "the south should not be changed to please the north, but should introduce change on its own merits". There was a need for a law in the Republic to deal with the legal consequences arising from marriage breakdown. He noted that there were also legal consequences for those who had obtained a decree of nullity from the Catholic Church's marriage tribunals, but had discovered that if they remarried in a Catholic Church they would be bigamous in the eyes of the State.

Mr Hume advised that if the political parties in the Republic agreed to the holding of a referendum to remove the constitutional ban on divorce, it would be futile to ask for a "yes" or a "no" answer. "You will get all kinds of extreme debating positions on this, highlighting the Californian divorce laws and other situations. So I am saying before you have a referendum, let the people know exactly what you are talking about. Let them know the exact specific law which would be proposed".

It was the Church's role in any society to deal with the ideal, and it was the State's role to deal with the real. "I believe what has been absent in this country is a real debate about the role of Church and State, a debate setting out the parameters. If that had been done first the problem of divorce could be dealt with in that context. The reality facing the State at the moment is that there is a huge problem of marriage break-down. Marriage breakdown has legal consequences. The State has a duty to face up to that responsibility and to deal with the legal consequences of marriage breakdown. The real question that has to be put to the people of Ireland is not whether or not to have a divorce law but what sort of law''.

According to Mr Hume the question boiled down to main-taining either the precepts of a confessional state or of allow-ing for pluralism and diversity. One of the consequences of the drawing of the border between the two parts of Ireland in 1920 was that it made worse the divisions between the two communities. Partition had increased the paranoia of unionists about Home Rule being Rome Rule and had made them more dependent on sectarian politics; it had resulted in the party political system in the Republic which had become increasingly Catholic in emphasis under Mr W T Cosgrave and Mr de Valera; and thirdly, it had created two sectarian States by separating the two communities the way it did. "I believe that the only way we are going to get back to a situa-tion in which we have a constitution and law which respects diversity and differences is when we begin to interact again".

Media attention that weekend focused on what was seen as Mr Cooney's challenge to Dr FitzGerald rather than on the clue from John Hume about how to approach a divorce referendum. The media were unwilling to give Dr FitzGerald's intentions the benefit of the doubt when he told a Fine Gael conference at Goffs, Co. Kildare on Sunday 8 December that the first stage of dealing with the injustices involved in marital breakdown must be a discussion of the matter between the State and the various Churches jointly. "I intend to initiate such consultations shortly", he said, making it publicly known that he would not proceed on the basis of the bill put forward by the Labour party.

Annoyed by Dr FitzGerald's dismissal of the Labour bill as "out of place and premature", the Labour chairman, Senator Michael D Higgins, claimed that the consultations with the Churches was quite clearly a diversionary tactic calculated to delay making a decision. "No amount of consultation will change the view of the Catholic Church on the issue of divorce, a view made clear by them on a number of occasions, and one indeed which they are perfectly entitled to hold".

Dr FitzGerald's decision to enter consultations of a denominational kind was grossly offensive to Labour, Mr Higgins said, serving notice that despite the confusion in Fine Gael, the Labour party would proceed with its bill in the Oireachtas at the earliest appropriate moment. In a side-swipe at Fianna Fáil, Mr Higgins observed that "the other major conservative party continues its enforced silence on all areas of social legislation and consolidating its truly anti-women stance".

The positive response in the Republic to the Anglo-Irish Agreement - and the abrupt initial dismissal of that Agreement by Mr Haughey - resulted in a resurgence of Dr FitzGerald's standing and a drop in the Fianna Fáil leader's popularity. An *Irish Times/MRBI* opinion poll showed a 52 - 42 per cent lead for those in favour of a referendum to remove the divorce ban. It also showed 77 per cent in favour of divorce in limited circumstances.

Just before Christmas Mr Desmond O'Malley and Ms Mary Harney formed the Progressive Democrats and promised and end to "Civil War" politics.

The Labour Bill

It was not until Tuesday 18 February 1986 that the Labour Divorce Bill was taken in the Dáil at Private Members' Time. This was the first time since the introduction of the constitution in 1937 that a bill to delete the ban on divorce had reached the second stage in the Dáil. Under the bill, the Oireachtas would be enabled to make provision for civil divorce subject to three conditions - that divorce could only be granted by a court, that the grounds for divorce would be irretrievable breakdown of the marriage, and that the needs of a dependent spouse and children were met.

Moving the second stage of the bill the party's chief whip, Mervyn Taylor, appealed for the people to be given the chance to vote on providing for the right of marriage to couples whose existing marriages were irretrievably broken down. Fianna Fáil's Justice spokesman, Dr Michael Woods, said his party was not against holding a referendum but that that would have to be done following a bill sponsored by the

116

government. For the government, the new Justice Minister, Alan Dukes, said that while he agreed with a great deal of what Mr Taylor had said it would be inappropriate in the light of the Taoseach's forthcoming talks with the Churches for the Dáil to engage in detailed debate on the merits of the bill. Mr Desmond O'Malley pledged the support of the Progressive Democrats for the second reading of the bill but announced that he would publish shortly substantive Divorce bill proposals. Mr O'Malley ridiculed Dr FitzGerald as being among "those constitutional crusaders prepared to fight any battle - so long as it is tomorrow".

An eloquent appeal for compassion towards those whose marriages had broken down was made by Mrs. Eileen Desmond.

"In many cases, desertion is a merciful end to years of terror, punishment and misery. As a woman public representative for more than 20 years I have had the confidence of women in my constituency and outside it and I have been shown all the marks of terrifying, brutal marriages - bruises, black eyes, broken fingers, burn marks. I have seen children in total terror, marked for life. I would judge that there are children who have been marked for life in what I would call the more civilised cases, where the fathers and mothers have not spoken to each other for years.

"This is what the State is now being urged to continue to batten down the hatches on. While battening down those hatches we conveniently turn a blind eye to all the Irish style solutions to which people have to resort, such as divorces by husbands who have domicile abroad while up to now a wife is supposed to have domicile with her husband. The wife is left to cope with her children back in Ireland though she is supposed to be wherever the husband is. He gets a divorce. We ignore Mexican divorces, Haitian divorces, the Puerto Rican divorces - they may be few, but they are there - the deed poll changing of names, Catholic Church annulments and subsequent Catholic Church second weddings.

The Minister for Health, Mr. Desmond, said the Labour Bill had helped to concentrate the mind of this house and of public opinion on the need for action. He had sufficient confidence in the strength of marriage and family life to argue that

117

divorce would never be a remedy for more than a minority of Ireland's half a million marriages. Ireland should take courage from Spain, which shared a firm attachment to Catholic teaching on marriage and the family. In the three years since divorce was introduced in Spain, some 50,000 couples had split up - well short of the 500,000 predicted by many. The hierarchy should be consulted about any changes proposed in marriage law. What he could not accept was that the Catholic Church should hold a veto over the introduction of civil divorce.

The Minister for Labour and the Public Service, Mr. Ruairí Quinn, said politicians had to bring to fruition an Irish Republic in which the Oireachtas was the place where laws were made and unmade and the church was the place where people went to pray and practice their religion. This would not be done until there was a clear distinction in the reality and the perception of ordinary men and women that there was a separation of Church and State.

Those who were worried that the fabric of Irish society would collapse if the bill were passed should look to countries like Portugal and Italy, with whom we had close affinities and where there was divorce but they did not experience any collapse of the kind feared here.

The other Fianna Fáil speaker was David Andrews, who said he supported the removal of the ban but felt the Labour Bill was defective in its wording. Once again the government was not governing and was allowing the Labour rump to carry the bill.

Mr Alan Shatter said he believed that the response of the Fine Gael party to the bill would be seen as the litmus test for those who espoused constitutional social reform. "Unless a significant number of members of the Fine Gael Parliamentary Party support the bill in the lobbies on a second stage vote, irreparable and permanent damage will be done to the Fine Gael Party and to the credibility of the party's commitment to social and constitutional reform", he said.

Mr Michael Bell, Labour deputy for Louth, said: "This house is running away from its constitutional responsibility and handing it over to all sorts of pressure groups".

Mr Michael O'Leary said Fine Gael should not refrain from

supporting the bill just because of the Church consultations by the Taoiseach. "The Taoiseach cannot reverse the decision of the Council of Trent. The Church has a settled view on the question of divorce", he said.

The only remaining possibility of a divorce referendum being held before the next election, now depended on the outcome of the Taoiseach's consultations with the Churches, following the failure of the Labour Party's divorce bill on 26 February 1986. The fourth attempt in the lifetime of the present Dáil to obtain approval for a divorce referendum, was defeated by 54 votes to 33, when only 11 Fine Gael deputies joined forces with Labour deputies. Fianna Fáil members abstained. The Bill, the Tenth Amendment to the Constitution, was also supported by the Progressive Democrats, the Workers Party and the Independent deputy, Mr. Tony Gregory.

Immediately after the vote, the Taoiseach said that he was pleased that the Dáil had decided not to pre-empt his consultation with the Churches. Only hours earlier, the Catholic bishops issued a statement affirming that they neither claimed nor sought a veto on the introduction of civil divorce.

The bishops' statement, which was a direct reply to the Minister for Health, Mr Desmond, was seen as a readiness by them to adopt an non-confrontational approach to the consultations with the Taoiseach on marriage and the family.

It was the understanding that Dr FitzGerald would bring forward proposals after Easter that persuaded most Fine Gael deputies to oppose the Labour Bill, despite a last-minute appeal by the Tanaiste, Mr Spring for all members to vote for the measure.

The Fine Gael deputies who voted for the bill were Mr Michael Keating, Mr Brendan McGahon, Ms Mary Flaherty, Ms Monica Barnes, Mr Alan Shatter, Mr Hugh Coveney, Mr Liam Skelly, Mr Maurice Manning, Mr Richard Bruton, Ms Nora Owen and Mr Michael O'Leary.

Enter the Churches

The ambitious intentions set by the Taoiseach in his talks with the churchmen became known publicly when on 28 February *The Irish Times* carried the details of his correspondence with the Catholic hierarchy, the Church of Ireland, the Presbyterian and Methodist Churches, the Jewish Community and the Religious Society of Friends (Quakers). Dr FitzGerald requested their views on eight areas of marriage' law.

These were: 1 The minimum age for marriage: The Joint Committee had urged raising this from 16 to 18 years.

2 Possible minimum period of notice before a marriage takes place: The commmittee advised that the State should ensure that the educational system should prepare the individual for marriage, and that anyone wishing to marry should have access to a premarriage guidance service.

3 Counselling for couples in marriage difficulties: The committee called for the provision of an easily accessible and effective counselling service.

4 Legal grounds for separation *A Mensa Et Thoro:* This is the decree of judicial separation based on proof of adultery, cruelty, or unnatural practices but which does not confer a right to remarry. The committee proposed that irretrievable breakdown should be the one overall ground for the granting of a judicial separation.

5 Enforcement of the law of bigamy: Catholics who obtain an ecclesiastical annulment and remarry in a church service are technically bigamous in State law.

6 Possible changes in the law of nullity: The Oireachtas committee called for the introduction of legislation to update the civil law of nullity. The Catholic bishops in their pastoral letter, *Love is for Life,* while favouring the updating of certain aspects of the civil law, argued that there must be strong resistance to making a nullity a form of backdoor divorce.

7 The possible establishment of family tribunals to deal with all types of marriage cases: The committee favoured a new family court structure, advocating the establishment of a body with full and exclusive powers to deal with all types of family cases, as part of the High Court.

8 Divorce *A Vinculo Matrimonii* (from the bond of marriage) and remarriage in cases where a marriage has irretrievably broken down.

The consultations began on 21 March when Dr FitzGerald, accompanied by the Minister for Justice, Mr Alan Dukes, held separate meetings at Government Buildings with the leaders of the Presbyterian Church, the Society of Friends (Quakers) and the Jewish Community. The common assumption of the three delegations was that the prohibition of divorce in the constitution reflected Catholic teaching and they urged Dr FitzGerald to take account of the different points of view in a pluralist society. They also asked the Taoiseach to recognise the need for divorce, distinguishing between their Churches' religious teaching upholding marriage as a sacred bond and the duty of the State to provide for the dissolution of marriages which had failed.

The high-level delegation from the Presbyterian Church included ministers from both the Republic and Northern Ireland, led by the Moderator of the General Assembly, the Rev Robert Dickinson. Speaking to reporters after the meeting, Dr Dickinson said: "What we are seeking is an equal opportunity for people of all denominations and none to have access to legal provision for the situation in which marriage breaks down".

Dr Dickinson said that while the Presbyterian Church was deeply committed to the sanctity of marriage, it did recognise that marriages did break down and that the State must make legal provision for that.

The Chief Rabbi, Dr Ephraim Mirvis, described his delegation's two-hour meeting with Dr FitzGerald as "thorough and very fruitful". He urged the Taoiseach to hold a referendum to remove the constitutional ban on divorce in the hope that the referendum would be carried and members of the Dáil and Senate would be empowered to introduce an appropriate divorce law. Dr Mirvis said that few things were as important in Judaism as its teaching on the sanctity of family life. But he acknowledged that divorce would be a blessing for those citizens suffering in marriages which had irretrievably broken down. The Jewish community supported the raising of the minimum age of marriage to 18, favoured a longer waiting period for engaged couples so they could better prepare for marriage and advocated the provision of better counselling services. The leader of the delegation from the Religious Society of Friends, Mr Maurice Wigham, said that Quakers recognised divorce as necessary in cases of complete marriage breakdown. Marriage dissolution was regarded by Quakers as a matter of Christian charity and concern.

On March 24th Dr FitzGerald and Mr Dukes met representatives from the Baptist and Methodist Churches. The leader of the Baptist delegation, Pastor Robert Dunlop, said that they had explained their Church's position on the separation of Church and State and had proposed that the civil marriage contract should be the responsibility of the civil power and the religious ceremony a matter for the Churches. The delegation from the Methodist Church was led by its president, the Rev Hamilton Skillen. A member of the group, the Rev Kenneth Thompson, said they had impressed on Dr FitzGerald their strong attachment to the permanence of marriage while recognising the difficulties caused by breakdown. They had suggested that the only realistic solution was the provision of divorce. They pressed for an early referendum.

They had pressed strongly for the civil registration of all marriages so that proper records could be kept to guard against bigamy and to differentiate between the civil and the religious ceremony. Mr Thompson said they had favoured the raising of the minimum age for marriage to 18 years and had found themselves very strongly in support of most of the recommendations made by the Joint Committee. They had pressed for greater State involvement in the provision of a countrywide marriage counselling service and had not favoured the extension of civil nullity as an answer to marital problems. They did not regard nullity as a way forward to any great extent and would not want to see it extended as a possible answer to the problem of marital breakdown because it left the question of children in a very unsatisfactory position, Mr Thompson said.

On Saturday 5 April Dr FitzGerald and Mr Dukes met a Church of Ireland delegation, headed by its new Primate, the Archbishop of Armagh, Dr Robin Eames, accompanied by the Archbishop of Dublin, Dr Donald Caird, and the Bishop of Meath and Kildare, Dr Walton Empey. The delegation told the Taoiseach that while there were circumstances in which divorce was the lesser of two evils, it should only be available in the event of "irretrievable breakdown".

122

The Catholic bishops

After a five hour meeting at Government Buildings on Monday 7 April, Cardinal Ó Fiaich said that the Catholic bishops were united in the belief that the introduction of even a limited form of divorce law in the Republic would be harmful to society. The Cardinal told reporters that the delegation had pointed out to the Taoiseach that it would be difficult to prevent even a very restrictive piece of legislation from growing into a "quicky" system of divorce. But he added that the Taoiseach had not sought the advice of the Catholic bishops on whether or not to hold a referendum to remove the constitutional prohibition on divorce. Nor would the episcopal delegation give advice on a matter which was entirely a political decision, he said.

"The Taoiseach will have to make up his mind", Cardinal Ó Fiaich said, describing the consultation on a wide range of marriage issues as "positive and constructive".

Cardinal Ó Fiaich noted that the outcome of a referendum would be influenced by whether the government proposed merely the removal of the constitutional ban on divorce or whether it also indicated the kind of divorce legislation it would intend bringing in. The Cardinal agreed that Dr FitzGerald had been coming under increased pressure from the public in favour of divorce but he felt that the polls were unclear and that it was hard to forecast how the electorate would vote.

While Cardinal Ó Fiaich was careful to stress that the bishops would not respond until they knew the form of the government proposal, it was clear from the consultations that the bishops were determined to exert their influence against any move to introduce divorce.

A 22 page document was presented to the Taoiseach, in which the bishops argued that divorce based on irretrievable breakdown severely damages the stability of marriage and has serious moral and social consequences.

The Cardinal said to reporters that the bishops would not be deflected from this opposition to divorce because the Protestants accepted a form of divorce. Nor did the Cardinal accept the argument that the introduction of divorce in the Republic would narrow differences with unionists in Northern Ireland and that it would help create a more pluralist climate for the development of the Anglo-Irish Agreement. "Protestant leaders have made it clear on several occasions - on contraception, on divorce and on moral issues - that no change will influence their political outlook", the Cardinal said.

The main message from the delegation to the Taoiseach was that "divorce legislation affects all marriages, not simply broken marriages", the Cardinal explained. From being a permanent contract, marriage tended to be seen as a temporary thing once divorce legislation was introduced.

Another important point stressed by the bishops was that the introduction of divorce would not be a solution to the situation of Catholics who had remarried after obtaining ecclesiastical annulments but were regarded as bigamous in the law of the State. Cardinal Ó Fiaich said that he thought that there was now a great amount of harmony between State law and the Catholic Church on the question of nullity as a result of recent developments in the law of civil annulments.

After intensive discussions - and at least a dozen drafts - Dr FitzGerald and Mr Spring announced the details of the government's proposals. There was a mood of relief around Leinster House that a decision had been made and that a campaign would be short but sharp.

EPILOGUE

Day of decision

On Saturday 19 October 1985 Garret FitzGerald invited journalists accompanying him to the United Nations in New York to lunch at the residence of the Irish Ambassador, Bob McDonagh. The conversation turned to the divorce issue. He was insistent that the climate was not yet right for a referendum and that there would have to be a consistent lead in the opinion polls in favour of the ban's repeal before it would be politically safe to tackle it. Otherwise the issue could be set back for a decade, if defeated.

On Sunday 8 December at Goff's Co. Kildare, Dr. FitzGerald announced his intention of consulting the Churches on marriage problems, the final hurdle before taking the political decision at government level about divorce. The change in the Taoiseach's outlook is due to the tremendous initial success which greeted the Anglo-Irish Agreement. The essential clue of his direction came in Dr. FitzGerald's contribution in the Senate debate on 27 November. In his own hand-writing he added to his prepared typed text the final passage:

"Towards the end of healing the divisions between nationalists and unionists, I believe that we must tackle aspects of our constitutional laws which represent an impediment to the establishment here of a pluralist society upon which basis alone we can credibly propose to Northern unionists in time a coming together in peace and by agreement and free consent of the two parts of Ireland".

It was the signal that the crusade which he had outlined in 1964 in *Studies,* which he expanded in his 1972 book *Towards a New Ireland,* which took him in 1973 and 1977 to the Vatican, which he had explained on RTÉ radio in September 1981, which had inspired him to set up the New Ireland Forum

125

and which had led to the Anglo-Irish Agreement with Mrs. Thatcher in November 1985, had selected the divorce referendum as the next goal.

The linkage between Dr. FitzGerald's divorce referendum and his Northern Ireland policy was highlighted by himself in his Dáil contribution on May 16th 1986 when he urged the electorate not to ignore the beneficial effect which the acceptance of divorce in the Republic could have in improving relations with Northern Ireland and between unionists and nationalists in the north at this delicate time.

While Dr FitzGerald still makes a linkage between pluralism in the Republic and Irish unity, he has come to recognise that changes in the south will not alter the views of Rev Ian Paisley and unionist leaders. Mr Peter Barry is more forthright on this than Dr FitzGerald. At a news conference on May 29, 1986, to launch the Fine Gael campaign, Mr Barry said that if the divorce referendum were lost, it would not have a disastrous effect on relationships between the Republic and Northern Ireland. Mr Barry also doubted that the people of Northern Ireland would see the outcome, if the referendum were defeated, as proof that the Republic is a Catholic state for a Catholic people.

In May 1986 the Dáil and Senate passed the enabling bill for a referendum seeking the removal of the ban on divorce. The Catholic bishops have declared themselves firmly against divorce. Thursday June 26th 1986 is the date for the people's choice between the Crozier and the Dáil.

BIBLIOGRAPHICAL NOTE

The original idea broached by Seán O Boyle was for a book containing contributions from the political leaders on their attitudes to Church-State relations. It proved difficult to obtain their immediate co-operation as the divorce issue was becoming such a live issue. When Dr. FitzGerald announced his divorce proposals and his plans for a referendum in June, I felt it was worth taking the gamble against time, family commitments and daily journalism to attempt to tell the story of the Church-State relationship since 1922.

In doing so I have benefited from conversations with *Irish Times* Political Editor, Dick Walsh, from *Irish Press* Religious Affairs Correspondent, T.P. O'Mahony and from Father Bernard Treacy OP. I have also benefited from conversations with "informed sources" who have made information available to me on an unattributable basis. The staff of *The Irish Times* library, as always, responded to my inquiries. I remain solely responsible for the book's contents.

In concentrating on the theme of pluralism/confessionalism, I am conscious of not giving attention to powerful formative agencies such as education and health. There is a need for these two themes to be treated separately and at length. In the historical sections I have leaned heavily on basic works by scholars whose work may not be so well known to the public.

A good outline of Church-State developments is sketched by Dr. Ronan Fanning in his *Independent Ireland* (Helicon 1983). See The Catholic Church and the Irish Free State (pages 53-60), The faith of the majority (pages 127-134), The Mother and Child Controversy (pages 181-187), the Relaxation of censorship and Vatican II (pages 200-202). For the 1953 Act see his two articles, *Fianna Fáil and the Bishops* in *The Irish Times*, February 13th and 14th, 1985. The two key scholarly books are Dr. J.H. Whyte's *Church and State in Modern Ireland 1923-1979*, (Gill & Macmillan) and Dr. Dermot Keogh's *The Vatican, the Bishops and Irish Politics 1919-39*, (Oxford University Press).

In his *The Politics of Dishonour: Ireland 1916-77*, T.P. O'Mahony gives an angry trenchant assessment of "the rocky road" to achieving pluralism in Ireland. It is a book which would be well worth the author's time updating.

Blanchard, Jean, *The Church in Contemporary Ireland* (1963) Burns and Oates.

Blanshard, Paul, *The Irish and Catholic Power* (1954) Verschoyle.

Browne, Terence, *Ireland, A Social and Cultural History* (1981) Fontana.

Falconer Alan, Editor, *Freedom to hope? - The Catholic Church in Ireland twenty years after Vatican II* (1985) Columba Press.

FitzGerald, Garret, *Towards a New Ireland* (1972) Gill & Macmillan.

Hurley, Michael, Editor, *Beyond Tolerance*, (1975) Chapman.

Kirby, Peadar, *Is Irish Catholicism dying?* (1984) Mercier.

Newman, Jeremiah, *Ireland must choose* (1983) Four Courts.

McDonagh, Enda, Editor, *Irish Challenges to Theology* (1986) Dominican Publications.

McNamara, Kevin, *Pluralism* (1986) Veritas.

O'Brien, Conor Cruise, *States of Ireland*, (1972) Hutchinson.

Smith, Raymond, *Garret the Enigma*, (1985), Aherlow.

Tobin, Fergal, *The Best of Decades: Ireland in the Sixties*. (1984) Gill and Macmillan.

Whyte, John, *Recent Developments in Church-State relations*, in *Journal of the Department of the Public Services*, Vol. 6. No.3. 1985.

1973 Statement of the Irish Episcopal Conference

The proposals which are currently being made to change the law on the sale of contraceptives in the Republic of Ireland raise an important issue for the people and for their elected representatives.

The question at issue is not whether artificial contraception is morally right or wrong. The clear teaching of the Catholic Church is that it is morally wrong. No change in State law can make the use of contraceptives morally right since what is wrong in itself remains wrong, regardless of what State law says.

It does not follow, of course, that the State is bound to prohibit the importation and sale of contraceptives. There are many things which the Catholic Church holds to be morally wrong and no one has ever suggested, least of all the Church herself, that they should be prohibited by the State.

Those who insist on seeing the issue purely in terms of the State enforcing, or not enforcing Catholic moral teaching, are therefore missing the point.

The real question facing the legislators is: What effect would the increased availability of contraceptives have on the quality of life in the Republic of Ireland?

That is a question of public, nor private morality. What the legislators have to decide is whether a change in the law would, on balance, do more harm than good, by damaging the character of the society for which they are responsible.

There is a good deal of evidence that it would. Experience elsewhere indicates that where the sale of contraceptives is legalised, marital infidelity increases, the birth of children outside of wedlock (surprising as it may seem) increases, abortions increase, there is a marked increase in the incidence of venereal disease and the use of contraceptives tends to spread rapidly among unmarried young people. [1]

The influence on young people is of particular significance because it affects the next generation of fathers and mothers. Legislation about the sale of contraceptives often contains provisions to safeguard against this and other abuses but experience shows that it is only a matter of time until such safeguards are eroded. Young people in Ireland have high moral standards but it may be felt that legislators ought to think very carefully before making the environment for moral living more difficult for them.

The link between legislation on contraception and abortion is also significant. Increasingly abortion is being seen as the ultimate method of birth control. There seems to be a chain-reaction in these matters by which the first piece of legislation tends to set in motion a process of change which no one can control.

Perhaps the most serious consideration of all is the effect which the contraceptive mentality has on the very way marriage and the family are looked upon in society. Once the gift of sex is seen as something that can be separated altogether from childbearing, people begin to ask what is the point of restricting it to marriage at all? Why should it be confined to a situation which is obviously designed for looking after children? The corrosive effect on the very concepts of marriage and the family which this contraceptive mentality has had in some Western societies, even in the few short years since the anovulant pill came to be used, is quite remarkable.

All these are factors which affect the quality of life in the society in which they are widespread. Sometimes a society, no less than the individual, has to impose rules of self-discipline on itself as a help towards preserving values which it holds dearly.

We emphasise that it is not a matter for bishops to decide whether the law should be changed or not. That is a matter for the legislators, after a conscientious consideration of all the factors involved.

What we are saying is that the factors outlined above are important and that they have tended to be overlooked in public discussion. They should be put into the balance, along with such other factors as the actual degree of inconvenience which the present law and practice causes to people of other religious persuasions, and a realistic assessment as to whether a change in the law would have any significant effect at the present time on attitudes towards the reunification of Ireland.

Next year we intend to publish a comprehensive pastoral letter on the sacredness of human life and its origins, seen in the light of the Church's vision of the family and society. In today's world faithfulness to the Gospel as proclaimed by the Church can, we are only too well aware, give rise to painful problems of an intimate nature within particular families, problems which call for Christian compassion and understanding within the Gospel message. The question with which this short statement is concerned - the question as to whether the present State law on the importation, sale and advertising of contraceptives should be relaxed - belongs to a different category of public rather than personal morality. Nevertheless an important moral issue is involved in it: the moral duty of legislators to weigh all the relevant factors conscientiously and impartially in coming to a decision which affects the common good.

The issue before the legislators and the people is therefore a grave one. People must try to weigh up all the issues fairly in their own minds, asking themselves what kind of society do they want, for themselves and their children.

† **John McCormack,**
Bishop of Meath,
Secretary.   **25th November, 1973.**

(1) In England and Wales the total number of illegitimate live births increased from 34,562 in 1957 to 65,678 in 1971 - despite the greatly increased sale of contraceptives during this period. In 1967 the illegitmate birth rate was even higher (69,928) but the introduction of legal abortion that year has resulted in less illegitimate babies being born alive. Thus in 1971, in addition to the 65,678 illegitimate live births, 52,932 women without husbands, and resident in England and Wales, had legal abortions.

131

Article of the Constitution

The Family.

Article 41.

1. 1 The State recognises the Family as the natural primary and fundamental unit group of Society, and as a moral institution possessing inalienable and imprescriptible rights, antecedent and superior to all positive law.

   2 The State, therefore, guarantees to protect the Family in its constitution and authority, as the necessary basis of social order and as indispensable to the welfare of the Nation and the State.

2. 1 In particular, the State recognises that by her life within the home, woman gives to the State a support without which the common good cannot be achieved.

   2 The State shall, therefore, endeavour to ensure that mothers shall not be obliged by economic necessity to engage in labour to the neglect of their duties in the home.

3. 1 The State pledges itself to guard with special care the institution of Marriage, on which the Family is founded, and to protect it against attack.

   2 No law shall be enacted providing for the grant of a dissolution of marriage.

   3 No person whose marriage has been dissolved under the civil law of any other State but is a subsisting valid marriage under the law for the time being in force within the jurisdiction of the Government and Parliament established by this Constitution shall be capable of contracting a valid marriage within that jurisdiction during the lifetime of the other party to the marriage so dissolved.

TENTH AMENDMENT OF THE CONSTITUTION BILL, 1986

BILL
entitled

AN ACT TO AMEND THE CONSTITUTION.

WHEREAS by virtue of Article 46 of the Constitution any provision 5 of the Constitution may be amended in the manner provided by that Article: 5

AND WHEREAS it is proposed to amend Article 41 of the Constitution:

BE IT THEREFORE ENACTED BY THE OIREACHTAS AS FOLLOWS: 10

Amendment of Article 41 of the Constitution.
1. - Article 41 of the Constitution is hereby amended as follows:
(a) the subsection set out in *Part I* of the Schedule to this Act shall be substituted for subsection 2° of section 3 of Article 41 of the Irish text,   15
(b) the subsection set out in *Part II* of the Schedule to this Act shall be substituted for subsection 2° of section 3 of Article 41 of the English text.

Citation.
2. - (1) The amendment of the Constitution effected by this Act shall be called the Tenth Amendment of the Constitution.   20

(2) This Act may be cited as the Tenth Amendment of the Constitution Act, 1986.

133

PART II

2° Where, and only where, such court established under this Constitution as may be prescribed by law is satisfied that -

15

    i. a marriage has failed,
    ii. the failure has continued for a period of, or periods amounting to, at least five years,
    iii. there is no reasonable possibility of reconciliation between the parties to the marriage, and

20

    iv. any other condition prescribed by law has been complied with,

the court may in accordance with the law grant a dissolution of the marriage that the court is satisfied that adequate and proper provision having regard to the circumstances will be made for any dependent spouse and for any child of or any child who is dependent on either spouse.

25

Statement on Government's Intentions with regard to Marriage, Separation and Divorce, 23rd April, 1986.

Referendum Bill

1. The government has published the 10th Amendment of the Constitution Bill 1986. The purpose of that Bill is to enable a Referendum to be held so that the people can decide whether or not they wish to remove the prohibition on the enactment by the Oireachtas of laws providing for divorce contained in Article 41.3.2. of the Constitution.

2. The purpose of this statement is to describe in broad terms the type of divorce legislation which the government would submit for the consideration of the Oireachtas if the proposal being put in the Referendum is approved by the people. That legislation will be designed to ensure that divorce will be available only in limited circumstances where a court is satisfied that the marriage has failed and that the failure has continued for a period or periods of not less than five years, and that adequate and proper provision, having regard to the circumstances, will be made for spouses and any dependent child of either party to the marriage.

3. The statement also sets out proposed changes in the arrangements for marriage and for judicial separation that will accompany the legislation mentioned in the previous paragraph.

Present Law - Separation

4. The legislation to be proposed will take account of certain procedures of the existing law.

5. Under the present law a married person may obtain a decree of divorce *a mensa et thoro* (judicial separation) which entitles that spouse to live separate and apart from

the other spouse, but not to remarry. Usually in connection with such a decree orders are also sought in relation to the custody of and access to the children of the marriage under the Guardianship of Infants Act, 1964 and in relation to maintenance of the spouse and dependent children under the Family Law (Maintenance of Spouses and Children) Act, 1976, and orders may be sought in relation to the family home.

6. Alternatively, married persons can enter into legally binding agreements enabling them to live separate and apart from each other and containing agreed provisions settling questions relating to maintenance, children and the ownership and occupation of the family home and other matters. Such an agreement may, on application to the Circuit Court or the High Court, under Section 8 of the Family Law (Maintenance of Spouses and Children) Act 1976 be made a rule of court if the court is satisfied that the agreement is a fair and reasonable one which in all the circumstances adequately protects the interests of both spouses and the dependent children (if any) of the family. The operation of the provisions of the Family Law (Maintenance of Spouses and Children) Act of 1976 may not be excluded or limited by such an agreement.

Changes in Legal Procedures for Separation

7. It is proposed to make a number of changes in the existing arrangements for judicial separation. First, such separations in future will be dealt with by a Family Court presided over by one of a number of judges of the Circuit court specially assigned for the purpose. Its procedures will be less formal and less confrontational than the procedures that exist at present. Cases heard in the Family Court will be heard *in camera*. Appeals from the Family Court will be to the High Court and will also be held *in camera*.

8. The Family Court will enquire into whether mediation services have been or should be availed of by the spouses to assist them in attempting a reconciliation and will have power to adjourn the proceedings so that recourse may be had to these services where it considers it necessary or

appropriate to do so. It is proposed that the mediation process be undertaken by registered counselling agencies - three such bodies exist at present which will be invited to undertake this work.

9. Where it emerges that no reconciliation of the partners to the existing marriage is possible, a conciliation process, designed to secure agreement between the parties in a non-confrontational manner on the terms of the separation, will then follow, to be undertaken either by the existing voluntary bodies, or, should these bodies prefer not to undertake this conciliation work on behalf of the court, through a conciliation service attached to the court itself.

10. The decision as to a judicial separation, and the terms of such a separation, will be determined by the court having heard the parties and any other appropriate evidence including a report on the results of this conciliation process.

11. As at present, separation agreements, entered into voluntarily by the two parties, can be made a rule of court if submitted to the Family Court, which before doing so must be satisfied that the agreement is a fair and reasonable one.

Changes in the Law on Judicial Separation

12. In conjunction with the changes in the procedure for judicial separation, changes will also be made in the *law* providing for judicial separation, the present grounds for which are cruelty, adultery and unnatural practices. In considering the changes to be made account has been taken of the recommendations made in the Law Reform Commission Report on Divorce *a mensa et thoro* and Related Matters, and in the Report of the Joint Committee of the Oireachtas on Marriage Breakdown. The additional grounds now proposed are desertion, including constructive desertion, (viz. conduct on the part of one spouse that results in the other spouse leaving and living apart); and separation for three years, or separation for one year with the consent of the respondent.

137

The final, and more general, ground proposed by the Committee, viz. that such other facts and/or reasons exist or existed which in all the circumstances make it reasonable for the applicant to live separate from and not cohabit with the other spouse, has not been adopted by the government. The government believes that the above grounds cover all appropriate cases, and that wording proposed by the Committee in this instance is unduly vague.

Financial Orders

13. The legislation will include provisions to enable the Family Court, on hearing an application for judicial separation or divorce, to make various financial orders with a view to ensuring that the interests of spouses and dependent children are adequately protected and appropriately provided for. These orders will relate to maintenance, lump sum payments and property owned by the spouses, including the family home. Consideration will be given to the recommendation of the Joint Oireachtas Committee that a dependent spouse should not be prejudiced in any determination of property rights by virtue of the fact that he or she gave up employment in the course of the marraige to attend to duties in the home.

    In the relevant areas of social policy the provision of support for families in distress will, in so far as possible, be made in a way that assists them in staying together and overcoming their difficulties. A review of existing policies will be made with this in mind.

Five-year Separation Pre-Condition - Form of Proposed Divorce Legislation

14. The divorce legislation to be proposed will require that before a spouse will be entitled to apply for a decree dissolving the marriage and enabling that spouse (and the other) to remarry, the spouses will first have availed themselves of either the separation procedures mentioned in paragraphs 10 and 11 above.

    A period or periods of not less than five years separation will be required before an application for divorce will be entertained. Provision will be made regulating the extent to which a period or periods or separation, occurring before the decree of judicial separation or rule of court, should be regarded as satisfying the five year period, but it will be provided that no decree of divorce will be granted within two years from the date of a judicial separation or the order making a separation agreement a rule of court. This will have the effect of ensuring that the arrangements made under the previous decree or rule of court in respect of a spouse or dependent children will have been in existence for a sufficient period, by the time a court comes to consider an application for divorce, to enable that court to have regard to their effectiveness.

15. The legislation will contain special provision to cater for cases where, at the passing of the legislation, spouses have been separated for long periods but may not have obtained decrees of judicial separation or had separation agreements made a rule of court. The government feel it would not be justifiable to require couples in that situation to obtain, after the commencement of the new legislation, a decree of judicial separation or an order making a separation agreement a rule of court and then wait a further lengthy period before presenting a petition for divorce. In these cases it will be possible to submit an application for divorce if the spouses can prove that they have been living apart for five years. In dealing with these cases the court will ensure that adequate arrangements are put in place for a spouse and dependent children of the marriage and will make whatever orders are necessary that their interests are protected.

Conditions for Granting Divorce Applications

16. Applications for divorce with the right to remarry will be made to the Family Court and heard *in camera*. A divorce may not be granted unless the court is satisfied:

    a. That the marriage has failed; that the failure has continued for a period or periods of at least five years, during which the parties have been separated in accordance wiith the separation procedures set out earlier; and that there is no reasonable possibility of a reconciliation between the parties.

b. That adequate and proper provision having regard to the circumstances has been made, and that it will be continued, for spouses and for any children dependent on either party of the marriage. The legislation will require the court to be furnished with a report on the physical and mental condition of the children and the court will have a discretion to order the separate representation of any children if it considers that necessary.

Spouses and Dependent Children

17. In relation to the last of these conditions, the government is concerned to ensure that any procedure for obtaining a divorce should be such as to ensure that the interests of spouses and dependent children are as fully proteced as is possible. Under the procedure proposed, questions relating to maintenance, children and property owned by the spouses including the family home will all have to come under the scrutiny of a court, either on an application for a decree of judicial separation or an application to have a separation or an application to have a separation agreement made a rule of court, long before a divorce petition comes to be submitted. Accordingly, arrangements will already have been made covering these matters, either by agreement of the parties or by direction of a court. When a petition for divorce is subsequently presented, the court will review the arrangements already in existence and make such variation in the arrangements as seems to it to be necessary to ensure that adequate and proper provision having regard to the circumstances has been made, and will be continued, for a spouse and dependent children.

Other Proposals

18. There are several other areas in which the government proposes to take action.

Law Relating to Marriage

19. The government proposes to change the law relating to

the minimum age of marriage. This age will in future be 18 with provision that the Family Court may authorise in exceptional circumstances the marriage of people between the ages of 16 and 18, having heard the parents.

20. The government also proposes to introduce a new requirement for a minimum period of notice of marriage. This minimum period of notice will be three months. The period may be abridged only with the consent of the Family Court, which may be given only where the court is satisfied that there are substantial grounds justifying such an abridgement.

Law of Nullity

21. It is proposed that the law relating to nullity of marriage will be reviewed, taking account of the recommendations contained in the Law Reform Commission's Report on Nullity of Marriage and the recommendations made by the Oireachtas Joint Committee on Marriage Breakdown.

Fianna Fáil Party Statement
25 April 1986

At a specially convened meeting today, the Fianna Fáil Parliamentary Party considered the proposal of the Coalition Government to seek the approval of the people for the alteration of Article 41 of the Constitution in order to allow for the dissolution of marriages in certain circumstances.

The party carefully considered all the many aspects and implications of this proposal and in particular its profound effect on the position of families and the nature and quality of our society. It also had regard to the many different but sincerely held views in the community on this issue and decided that the question should be left to the people as a whole to decide. Accordingly, the Party will not oppose, in the Dáil or Seanad, the proposal to hold a referendum.

Fianna Fáil would hope that this important issue will be fully and responsibily assessed by the people and a wise decision arrived at after an informed and balanced debate, free of rancour or prejudice. To ensure that the debate does not take place along party political lines, Fianna Fáil have decided that the party will not campaign politically in the referendum. Because, however, many members of the party feel deeply about the issue, individual deputies and senators will be free to participate personally in whatever way they wish in their individual capacities.

The family, under the constitution, is the natural primary and fundamental unit of society, which the State guarantees to protect. The State is also pledged to guard with special care the institution of marriage, on which the family is founded. Fianna Fáil are convinced that the stability of our society and the welfare of the individual can best be protected by adhering to these principles in the constitution and will press the government to implement, as a matter of urgency, a comprehensive programme of measures to support and sustain marriage and family as outlined in the Report of the Committee on Marital Breakdown.

The initial statement on the government's proposals with regard to Marriage, Separation and Divorce by the four Archbishops in the name of the Irish hierarchy Saturday 26 April 1986

Marital breakdown in our society is a distressing and growing problem. Through its pastoral ministry, the Catholic Church seeks in many ways to give practical expression to its compassion for those who suffer in this situation.

The proposals relating to marital breakdown published by the government in recent days include a number of useful initiatives, for instance, those concerned with the introduction of a Family Court, mediation and conciliation, the age of marriage and the requirement of a minimum period of notice.

While these proposals are welcome, it is regrettable that in the government statement on Wednesday, 23rd April they are linked with the introduction of a divorce law. We wish to make a number of comments on this aspect of the government's proposals:

1) The fundamental law of the State is a matter for the people and it is right that the people should have an opportunity to speak on a matter of this importance.

2) We recognise that many tragic problems arise in the context of marital breakdown. To alleviate these problems much improved legal provision is needed for mediation and conciliation, maintenance, custody of and access to children, the status of children, succession and legal separation. All this should be provided, and could be provided without the introduction of divorce.

3) It will be suggested that the proposal envisages a very restricted form of divorce. It is true that the granting of a divorce decree will be delayed, but the *grounds* suggested could scarcely be broader. "Failure" of a marriage is in fact the basis for the most advanced and most unrestrictive form of divorce in the world today.

4) Nowadays, in situations of failure in life it tends to be taken for granted that people should be given a "second chance". It is understandable that people are tempted to apply the same kind of considerations to a "failed" marriage. But in the case of marriage it must be asked what the giving of a second chance would imply. It would mean bringing the situation where, as far as the civil law was concerned, the phrase "till death do us part" or "as long as we both shall live" would always be deemed to include the added clause "or until one of us decides that the marriage has failed". Civil law would cease to recognise any marriage as indissoluble.

5) A national debate of fundamental importance for the future of our society is now opened. We emphasise that in this debate opposing views should be fairly stated and honestly listened to and appraised.

6) In the meantime, we ask all our people to pray earnestly that God may direct them in their thinking and in their ultimate choice.